MRS. SIMMS' FUN COOKING GUIDE

Mrs. Simms'
FUN COOKING GUIDE

Myrtle Landry Simms

PELICAN PUBLISHING COMPANY
Gretna 2001

First edition, 1966
First Pelican edition, 2001

The word "Pelican" and the depiction of a pelican are trademarks of Pelican Publishing Company, Inc., and are registered in the U.S. Patent and Trademark Office.

Library of Congress Cataloging-in-Publication Data

Simms, Myrtle Landry.
  Mrs. Simms' fun cooking guide / Myrtle Landry Simms.
    p. cm.
  Reprint. Originally published: Houston? : The Author, 1966.
  ISBN 1-56554-841-8
    1. Cookery, American—Louisiana style. 2. Cookery, Creole. 3. Cookery, Cajun. I. Title.

TX715.2.L68 S56 2001
641.5—dc21

00-069866

Printed in Canada

Published by Pelican Publishing Company, Inc.
1000 Burmaster Street, Gretna, Louisiana 70053

NOTES

When "half a shell of beaten egg" is mentioned, this means that the egg is broken, beaten, then replaced in one-half of the shell of the egg as a measure. This is an old Acadian habit. Utensils were few and means of measuring were "provincial". My mother taught this to me. Bless her memory!

Sauté is an Anglicized expression borrowed from the French of excellent cuisine. It means to fry lightly.

The use of teaspoon and tablespoon instead of the correct teaspoonful or tablespoonfuls is adopted to keep in line with cookery parlance.

To enhance the taste of the lowly fried egg, dash on it one drop of Tabasco pepper sauce. This is an everlasting New Orleans custom. One Louisiana Congressman nearly made it a congressional issue because Tabasco was absent from the breakfast table.

To be considered a "haut gourmet" when dessert is brought, try adding two or three teaspoons of black, unsweetened coffee in your ice cream. DELICIEUX !

Gumbo filé is a powdered herb made from dried leaves of the sassafras tree. It adds zest to gravies, sauces, and gumbo as no other herb can. It is both a tree and a shrub.

I cannot refrain from making a few remarks about this wonderful tree. It is at home in the kitchen, the laboratory, into perfume bottles, and beverages. From its volatile oils, perfume is made; from its roots, a tea is made, reputed to be a good spring tonic (its bark is also used for teas); and bitters and flavoring agents are made from its oils. And here you are putting it into foods! What other tree can make that boast?

Learn to cook with wines. You will be a popular hostess. The alcoholic content of wine evaporates in cooking, and it is the residue that gives the zing to your cooking.

FOREWORD

Myrtle Landry Simms comes from a family of cooks and restaurateurs. Members of the Landry family are founders and operators of a well-known chain of Louisiana restaurants. As a member of this clan, Mrs. Simms has created one of the outstanding seafood dishes—stuffed flounder—featured on the menus of these restaurants.

"Cooking in several languages" comes naturally to Myrtle Landry Simms. Descended on her mother's side from Acadian refugees from Nova Scotia and on her father's side from French immigrants, she is a Native of Southwest Louisiana. Thus she is familiar with the traditional dishes of Acadian cookery and of Creole cuisine, as well as of American food preparation in general.

Mrs. Simms has consistently proved a winner in cooking competitions in the Creole Cooking Contest of the annual International Rice Festival at Crowley, Louisiana; her rice, seafood, meat, and dessert dishes have received ribbons. Tops in these honors, the Tricolor ribbon, or sweepstakes award, was given to her in 1958 for her preparation of stuffed flounder.

Not surprisingly, people kept asking for the secret of her success. Obligingly, she tried to tell them. One secret, she confided, lay in her use of spices. "Spices should enhance but not disguise," she explained. But that answer was not enough to satisfy the askers. Friends and strangers begged for her special recipes. That's why, at last, she wrote a cookbook.

The FUN COOKING GUIDE was originally designed for the homemaker. The recipes set forth here are meant to help the good but economical cook and a relaxed hostess. Many of these recipes can be made up ahead of time and chilled until time to pop them into the oven or carry them to the dining table.

But this cookbook should not be reserved for the beginning homemaker. Anyone can use it and have fun doing so. The author invites cooks experienced and inexperienced to try her cooking techniques and "Be a guest at your own party!"

Bernice Larson Webb

ABOUT MRS. SIMMS

This is a good time to call special attention to a very special lady. This lady was quietly yet consistently an important part of the rice, fish, and cooking industry in both Lafayette and the state of Louisiana for so many years.

Myrtle Cecile Landry Simms was known for her delicious recipes and rice cookery. Her father, Alzace Landry, had eleven children: Eunice, Ada, Willie, Myrtle, Don, Stella, Lily, Rita, Ashby, Margaret, and Roland. He owned a meat market and made wonderful hogshead cheese, boudin, and andouille sausage. People came from all over to buy these great Cajun delicacies. "Papa" built a lean-to shed behind the meat market and started barbecuing using his wonderful "$1,000,000.00 Bar-B-Q Sauce." He put sawdust on the floor and picnic tables outside. He had his daughter-in-law Maude and his daughter Myrtle helping him. With Maude, Myrtle would cook the vegetables and corn bread at their home three blocks away, where Myrtle was born, and bring the food to the market and serve plate lunches there.

Later Papa's eyes began to go bad and he turned the meat market over to his son Willie, who had been working with him there. His son Don took over the restaurant portion, constructed a larger building, and changed the name to Don's Seafood Inn. They began serving seafood in addition to barbecue.

Myrtle helped in the restaurant as cashier, and in the kitchen she helped develop wonderful dishes such as stuffed flounder and shrimp gumbo. During this time she entered many contests, including at the Crowley Rice Festival, the Breaux Bridge Crawfish Festival, and others throughout the state.

Her brother Don was drafted in the service and Ashby took over and ran the restaurant until Don was discharged. Willie was also drafted during World War II, so his wife, Maude, ran the meat market. After they came out of the service the three of them formed a corporation, renaming the restaurant Don's Seafood and Steak House. Later Roland and Lily Landry Domingue came into the business as partners, opening the second Don's, in Baton Rouge. After that, other locations followed in New Orleans, Shreveport, Morgan City, Hammond, Monroe, Dallas, Houston, and Beaumont.

FISH COURTBOUILLON
(French for short bouillon)

(Serves 4)

1½ pound to 2 pounds your choice of fish cut in serving pieces, catfish, perch, brim, salmon, red fish, red snapper or so many others
Salt and Red pepper
2 or 3 cloves garlic minced
⅓ cup cooking oil
½ cup all-purpose flour
1 medium onion chopped fine
1 cup whole tomato chopped
½ cup tomato sauce
2 quarts water
1 bay leaf
1 stick celery
A pinch of oregano
1 tablespoon chopped parsley
1 tablespoon chopped green onion tops
A jigger of sherry wine (optional)
Half a lemon, sliced

Season fish generously with salt, pepper and garlic; put in a covered dish and chill many hours before cooking.

Make a roux by heating oil in a large heavy-bottomed pot, add flour, stir constantly, cooking over low heat until a reddish brown. Remove from heat for fear of burning; add onion, stir almost constantly, cook 4 or 5 minutes, return to heat, add tomatoes, cook over low heat 15 to 20 minutes, add bay leaf and water, stir; when it comes to a hard boil, reduce heat to low, cover pot with a tight-fitting lid and simmer 45 minutes, add fish and lemon; simmer about 1 hour longer.

When ready to serve, add parsley, green onion, and wine, cook 1 minute longer. Serve on soup plates with a scoop of cooked rice.

*FUN COOKING GUIDE: Flavor will improve if bouillon is made a few hours before serving; just heat thoroughly, then add onion, parsley and wine.

*FUN COOKING GUIDE: Many kinds of fish can be used in the court-bouillon, such as red snapper, red fish, gaspergou, or salmon.

CRABMEAT STUFFED EGGPLANT

(2 Servings)

1 eggplant, weighing about
   1½ to 2 pounds
½ pound cooked crabmeat
2 tablespoons butter
¼ cup water
2 tablespoons cooking oil
1 medium onion chopped fine
2 tablespoons chopped celery
1 clove garlic, mashed
½ teaspoon cayenne pepper
   for topping

2 slices very stale bread;
   soaked in ½ cup milk
½ shell of one beaten egg
   reserve other half for
   another use.
Pinch of oregano
Pinch of thyme
2 tablespoons cracker crumbs
   for filling
2 tablespoons cracker crumbs

Cut eggplant in half lengthwise. To make eggplant shell, start cutting around edges with a paring knife. Cut down to ¼ inch.

Continue by scooping out all pulp with a teaspoon, being careful not to break shell. Set aside.

In a quart of salted water, place eggplant shell, cut side down; cover and cook 10 minutes. Drain; grease around skin, place shell in shallow baking dish.

Cut the eggplant pulp in small pieces. Place eggplant, water, and butter in a stew pan; cover and cook over very low heat 15 minutes or until tender; stir occasionally. Uncover and cook out moisture (about 5 minutes). In another small stew pan, cook onion, celery, and garlic in oil until tender, about 5 minutes, stirring constantly; add soaked bread, cook and stir until glossy.

Add cooked eggplant; stir well. Season with oregano, thyme, salt, and pepper and set aside to cool.

When cool, add beaten egg, cracker crumbs, and crabmeat; season again if needed.

Spoon mixture into shells; sprinkle with cracker crumbs.

Preheat oven 350°. Bake 20 minutes. Flavor will improve, however, if stuffed eggplant is chilled many hours before baking.

*FUN COOKING GUIDE: Instead of crabmeat, shrimp may be used, or, for extra glamour, use both crabmeat and shrimp. Add raw shrimp to cooked eggplant pulp and cook 5 minutes longer.

STUFFED CRABS

(2 Servings)

1½ cups crabmeat
4 tablespoons butter or
  margarine
1 small onion, finely chopped
¼ cup chopped celery
1 clove garlic, mashed
2 slices of very stale bread;
  soaked in ½ cup of milk
1 very well beaten egg
½ teaspoon salt

A few drops Tabasco sauce
Pinch clove powder
pinch oregano
2 tablespoons cracker meal
1 tablespoon chopped green
  onion
1 tablespoon chopped parsley
2 tablespoons cracker or
  bread crumbs

Butter 4 crab shells, individual ramekins, or 1 casserole.

Cook onion, celery and garlic in the butter until tender, stirring constantly (should be done in 5 minutes); add moistened bread, clove, oregano, Tabasco sauce, salt and pepper; stir and cook about 5 minutes or until mixture becomes glossy. Add beaten egg, cook about 3 minutes, stirring constantly; cool.

Add crab meat to the cooked mixture; fold in, do not mash. Spoon crabmeat mixture into shells, ramekins, or casserole. Bake in preheated oven at 350° for 20 minutes.

*FUN COOKING GUIDE: If prepared and kept covered in refrigerator until time to bake, flavor will improve.

CRAYFISH STEW
(4 Servings)

1½ cup crayfish tails
¼ cup cooking oil
¼ cup all-purpose flour
1 small onion, chopped
1 stick celery, chopped
1 clove garlic, mashed
1 bay leaf
¾ cup whole tomatoes, canned
  or fresh, chopped

1½ pint cold water
1 pint cold water mixed with
½ cup crayfish fat
1 teaspoon salt
¼ teaspoon sugar
¼ teaspoon, red pepper
1 tablespoon green onion
1 tablespoon chopped parsley

In a heavy-bottomed pot, make a roux by adding flour to heated oil over low heat. Stir constantly until a deep golden brown; take pot away from heat for fear of burning. Add onion, garlic and celery; cook about 5 minutes or until tender; stir; return to heat and add 1 pint of water, tomatoes, sugar, salt and pepper; cook over high heat, stirring until sauce simmers; then reduce heat again.

While sauce is simmering, combine remaining water with crayfish fat in a large saucepan, cook over high heat, stirring constantly until it comes to a boil.

Add sauce to fat and water; let simmer 1 hour. Season with salt and pepper again if needed. Add crayfish tails, green onion, and parsley. Serve in soup plate over a scoop of cooked rice.

*FUN COOKING GUIDE: Crayfish stew improves in flavor if made ahead of serving time, and chilled. However, do not add crayfish tails, parsley, and green onions until ready to serve.

Crayfish tails toughen and get dark if overcooked, only cook 5 minutes, they are somewhat like egg, shrimp, and oysters.

Crayfish bisque

*FUN COOKING GUIDE: Make recipe as for fried bisque heads; only bake them about 15 minutes in a 350° oven. Add to stew above. Serve over cooked rice. Use about 4 stuffed heads per serving.

FRIED CRAYFISH BISQUE HEADS

1½ cup crayfish tails, cut in
  small pieces
25 more or less, crayfish heads
3 tablespoons butter or
  margarine
1 medium onion, chopped
1 stick celery, chopped
1 clove garlic, mashed
1 teaspoon salt
½ teaspoon red pepper

2 slices stale bread, soaked in
  ¼ cup milk
2 tablespoons of well
  beaten egg
⅓ cup water, mixed with
  crayfish fat
¾ cup cracker crumbs
1 more tablespoon butter
2 tablespoons Parmesan
  cheese

Cook onion, celery, and garlic in butter over medium heat until tender, stirring occasionally; add bread soaked in milk; stir until glossy and bread leaves the pot clean; stir in the egg; add salt and pepper, set aside to cool.

In another saucepan, heat water, crayfish fat and remaining butter; cool to lukewarm, then add cracker crumbs; stir into the cooked onion and bread mixture, beat until smooth, then add crayfish tails; mix well. Season again if needed. Add Parmesan cheese. Stuff crayfish heads with the mixture then fry.

Coating for frying:

½ cup all-purpose flour
1 egg, mixed with

3 tablespoons milk
½ cup cracker meal or crumbs

Coat all the heads with flour, then with well beaten egg and milk; then with cracker meal. Fry them in deep fat.

*FUN COOKING GUIDE: After the crayfish bisque heads are fixed ready to fry, they can be chilled many hours before frying.

*FUN COOKING GUIDE: For crayfish bisque to be served in stew, bake, then chill until ready to be served; Add to stew and heat through.

JAMBALAYA

(4 Servings)

1 cup crayfish tails
1 cup raw rice
2 cups water with crayfish fat
1 teaspoon salt
¾ cup whole canned tomatoes,
   chopped into small pieces
3 tablespoons cooking oil
1½ tablespoons all-purpose flour
1 medium onion chopped;
   divide in 2 portions

1 stick celery, chopped fine
1 Clove garlic, mashed
3 tablespoons butter
A pinch oregano
A pinch nutmeg
2 teaspoons chopped parsley
2 teaspoons chopped green
   onion

Use a large heavy-bottomed pot. Make a roux by adding flour to hot oil, over medium heat; stir constantly until golden brown. Take pot off heat for fear of burning. Quickly add onion, stirring constantly, until soft; add garlic, celery, tomatoes, salt, and rice. Put pot back over medium heat, stirring constantly. Add water, stirring until it comes to a hard boil. Cover with a tight-fitting lid, and reduce heat to very low; cook about 25 minutes, stirring occasionally with a fork, to prevent sticking.

In the meantime, while rice is cooking, sauté remaining onion in butter. Add crayfish tails; do not overcook or they will toughen. Cook 2 or 3 minutes, stirring constantly. Add oregano, nutmeg and ½ teaspoon salt.

After rice mixture is cooked, add cooked crayfish to rice; mix well. Cook about 5 minutes longer. Just before serving add parsley and green onion.

CRAYFISH PIE

Pie dough enough for 4 individual
   pies (or 2 large)
1½ cups crayfish tails; crayfish
   fat and water to make 2 cups
2 tablespoons butter
Salt and red pepper to taste
Pinch thyme
Pinch nutmeg
4 tablespoons cornstarch

3 tablespoons cooking oil
1 medium onion, chopped fine
¼ cup chopped celery
1 clove garlic, mashed
⅓ cup tomato sauce
   mixed with ⅓ cup water
1 tablespoon green onion
1 tablespoon parsley

Cook onion, celery, and garlic in cooking oil, stirring until tender. Dish out half the cooked mixture.

To the mixture, add tomato sauce, water, and crayfish fat, cook over medium heat and when it boils, slowly add cornstarch and water stirring until sauce thickens, season with nutmeg, thyme, red pepper, and salt to taste; set aside.

To the remaining cooked onion mixture in a saucepan add crayfish tails, butter, cook 2 to 3 minutes. Combine sauce, crayfish, green onion, and parsley. Cool then pour into 4 pastry lined pie plates, equally divided, wet edges of under crust, cover with upper crust, press edges together; prick with a fork. Bake in a 450° preheated oven 5 minutes; reduce heat to 400° and bake about 15 minutes longer.

*FUN COOKING GUIDE: Be a guest at your own party and prepare these ahead and chill before baking.

FILE GUMBO

(4 Servings)

1½ cups crayfish tails	1 stick celery, chopped
2 tablespoons butter	Salt and pepper to taste
Crayfish fat and water to make 3½ pints	1 bay leaf
¼ cup cooking oil	1 tablespoon chopped parsley
¼ cup all-purpose flour	1 tablespoon chopped green onion tops
1 medium onion, chopped	Gumbo filé (Herb made from sassafras leaves)
1 clove garlic, mashed	
1 cup whole tomatoes, chopped (canned or fresh)	

In a large pot with a heavy bottom, make a roux by adding flour to heated oil; cook over medium heat, stirring constantly until deep golden brown. Take pot off the heat, for fear of burning. Add onion, garlic, and celery; stir and cook until soft (3 to 4 minutes). Return to heat and add tomatoes; cook 5 minutes. Add fat and water and bay leaf. Stir until it comes to a hard boil. Reduce heat to simmer.

Salt and pepper to taste. Cover with a tight-fitting lid and cook 1 hour.

In a saucepan put butter, parsley, green onion, and tails. Cook about 2 or 3 minutes, then add to gumbo.

Serve in soup plates with hot cooked rice and ½ teaspoon filé per serving.

*FUN COOKING GUIDE: Be a guest at your own party! Make gumbo hours ahead of serving time, but do not add crayfish tail mixture, as they would get dark and tough. Heat and add just before serving. Gumbo will improve in flavor.

SHRIMPBOAT COCKTAIL

(4 Servings)

1 pound Gulf shrimp, raw	**1 tablespoon shredded celery**
1 pint water	**2 teaspoon salt**

In a small saucepan, boil water with salt and celery added; add shrimp, cook 5 minutes or only until shrimp turn pink; drain off liquid; cover pan with lid and cool shrimp. Peel and devein.

(Make Sauce)

In a small bowl combine:

½ **teaspoon salt**	½ **teaspoon celery salt**
1 teaspoon sugar	**1 teaspoon paprika**
½ **teaspoon onion salt**	**1 teaspoon prepared mustard**

Add the following ingredients alternately to the above ½ cup salad oil, ¼ cup apple cider vinegar. Dressing will thicken.

Combine sauce, shrimp, 1 medium onion sliced thin, half a lemon sliced thin, a tablespoon chopped parsley, 2 tablespoons capers, chopped.

Mix and put all in a covered dish, let steep in marinade 24 hours in refrigerator.

*FUN COOKING GUIDE: May marinate crabmeat in same kind of sauce, steep in marinade 24 hours.

TOP-OF-STOVE BAR-B-Q'D SHRIMP

(2 Servings)

½ **pound raw shrimp; peeled and devein**	**1 teaspoon catsup**
1 tablespoon cooking oil	¼ **teaspoon each paprika and oregano**
2 tablespoons vinegar	**1 drop smoke liquid (can be bought in groceries)**
1 teaspoon salt	
½ **teaspoon red pepper**	**Half a small onion minced**
½ **teaspoon sugar**	**1 clove garlic minced**

Marinate the shrimp in all of the ingredients in a covered dish; keep in refrigerator for several hours, tossing occasionally. Drain off liquid and put seasoned shrimp in a saucepan with 4 table-spoons cooking oil; cook over medium heat 10 minutes or until shrimp turn pink. Serve hot.

*FUN COOKING GUIDE: Fresh shrimp can be marinated with head and peel left on, then Bar-B-Q'd for a taste treat.

LOUISIANA FRENCH OYSTER LOAF

1 large French bread
¼ cup melted butter or
   margarine

1 dozen raw oysters; drain
   off liquid
Yellow corn meal.

Preheat oven 400°

Cut through ⅓ of the top of the bread loaf. Hollow out the inside, leaving only the crust. Brush inside and out with melted butter. Wrap completely with aluminum foil. Set aside.

Season oysters with salt and pepper. Coat them with corn meal; heat cooking oil. Fry oysters in hot fat till golden brown. Drain on a paper towel.

While oysters are frying, heat loaf of bread 8 to 10 minutes. Fill loaf with fried oysters. Serve lettuce, tomatoes, pickles, or catsup separately.

*FUN COOKING GUIDE: Shrimp loaf is good also. Peel, devein, season, and fry shrimp, in the same manner as oysters.

POMPANO-EN-PAPILLOTTE

(Serves 2)

½ cup crabmeat
1 pound fillet of pompano
4 tablespoon butter
1 small onion, chopped fine
1 stick celery, chopped fine
2 tablespoons flour
½ cup milk
1 tablespoon sherry wine
   (optional)
juice of a half a lemon

½ shell of a beaten egg
½ cup cracker crumbs
Salt and red pepper to taste
¼ teaspoon ground ginger
1 teaspoon chopped green
   onion
1 teaspoon chopped parsley
2 pieces of parchment paper
   or aluminum foil

Season pompano with salt and pepper; put in a covered dish in refrigerator 2 or 3 hours.

Cook onion and celery in butter over low heat, stirring, until tender, stir in the flour, blend well, add milk; cook and stir until mixture thickens. Pour mixture in a bowl. Cool.

To the cooled mixture, combine with ginger, egg, cracker crumbs, parsley, green onions, and wine, beat well and fold in the crabmeat. Divide the fish into 2 equal parts, place half on buttered pieces of paper or foil, spoon crabmeat filling over each and spread evenly, place other halves of fish over filling, squeeze lemon over top, then dot with butter.

Fold paper or foil over, seal all around, crimping the edges together, to make package airtight.

Arrange the papillottes on a baking sheet, and bake in a 350° preheated oven 20 or 25 minutes. Serve fish in their envelopes; garnish with lemon wedges.

*FUN COOKING GUIDE: Be a guest at your own party; multiply for larger quantities. Make ahead, chill, then bake when ready to serve.

*FUN COOKING GUIDE: Any tender fish fillet can be used such as flounder or your choice of tender fish.

SEAFOOD CASSEROLE

(4 Servings)

1½ cups crabmeat
2 dozen oysters; heated in
    own juice, drain
½ pound shrimp; peeled and
    deveined
2 tablespoons butter or
    margarine

1 small onion, minced
1 clove garlic, mashed
    juice from half a lemon
Pinch nutmeg
½ cup cracker crumbs
American or Velveeta cheese,
    grated

In a saucepan over medium heat, add butter, onion and garlic; cook until tender; then add shrimp; cook 4 or 5 minutes or until they turn pink; season with salt and pepper; set aside to cool.

In a bowl, combine drained oysters and shrimp mixture; crabmeat, lemon juice and nutmeg. Salt and pepper to taste; set aside.

Prepare sauce for casserole

2 tablespoons butter
2 tablespoons all purpose flour
1 cup milk; sweet

½ teaspoon salt
2 drops Tabasco sauce

In a small saucepan, add butter, melt over low heat; blend in the flour, then gradually add milk, stirring until smooth; season with salt and Tabasco sauce.

Butter a small baking dish, in alternate layers, arrange half combined mixture of seafood, then half the cream sauce; cracker crumbs; grated cheese; continue with a second layer of seafood, sauce, cracker crumbs and cheese. Bake in a preheated over 350°F 20 minutes.

*FUN COOKING GUIDE: Be a guest at your own party. Prepare this dish hours ahead; chill, then bake 25 minutes.

SHRIMP CREOLE

(2 Servings)

½ pound fresh shrimp, peeled, deveined and washed
1 bay leaf
¼ lemon
1½ cups water
1½ tablespoons cooking oil
1 small onion, chopped
1 clove garlic, mashed
1 cup whole tomatoes, fresh or canned
½ cup tomato sauce
Liquid from boiled shrimp
½ teaspoon sugar
A small piece of bell pepper, cut fine
⅛ teaspoon sweet basil
pinch nutmeg
small piece of bayleaf
⅛ teaspoon red pepper
½ teaspoon cornstarch
A small amount of chopped parsley
A small amount of green onion

In a stew pan, add water, salt, bay leaf, lemon, and shrimp. Cook over medium heat. When water comes to a boil, cover and cook 5 minutes. Drain and reserve liquid.

Sauté onion and garlic in oil until tender, add tomatoes, shrimp broth, sugar, and bell pepper, reduce heat and simmer 15 minutes. Add sweet basil, nutmeg, red pepper, and salt to taste; cook a few minutes more.

Make a paste with corn starch and 2 tablespoons water. Stir it into the sauce; stir and cook until it thickens. When ready to serve, add the boiled shrimp, parsley, and green onion. Serve with cooked rice.

*FUN COOKING GUIDE: For improved flavor, cook shrimp, and make sauce, but do not add shrimp to sauce until ready to serve, chill. Be a guest.

SHRIMP AND OKRA GUMBO

(4 servings)

1 pound fresh shrimp, peeled and deveined
¼ cup cooking oil
1 piece bell pepper, cut in small pieces
1 piece bay leaf
1 stick celery, chopped
½ pound fresh or frozen okra cut in small pieces
1 clove garlic, mashed
⅓ cup all-purpose flour
1 medium onion, chopped
¾ cup whole tomatoes,
1 tablespoon chopped green onion
1 tablespoon chopped parsley
3½ pints water with shrimp broth
Salt
Red Pepper

Put fresh shrimp in 1 pint of water with 1 teaspoon salt, cook over medium heat about 5 minutes or until shrimp turns pink. Turn off heat and leave covered 3 minutes, drain and reserve liquid for gumbo.

In a large pot with heavy bottom, add flour to heated oil. Cook and stir constantly, until a deep golden brown. Take pot away from heat, and quickly add onion and garlic; cook 4 minutes; return to heat; add bell pepper, bay leaf, broth with remaining water and dried shrimp (optional). Let come to a boil, then add tomatoes and okra, stirring until it comes to a boil again, then reduce to simmer and cook 1 hour, covered with a lid.

Add cooked shrimp, green onion, and parsley to gumbo just before serving. Serve in soup plates with cooked rice.

*FUN COOKING GUIDE: Add a chopped hard-boiled egg for a taste treat. May use a few dried shrimp for extra flavor.

*FUN COOKING GUIDE: For a different taste treat, shrimp gumbo filé is made the same way, only omit the okra, but put 1/4 teaspoon gumbo filé into each serving. Gumbo filé is a hero powder made from sassafras leaves, to be found in most spice sections in stores.

FRIED SHRIMP

(2 Servings)

1/2 **pound shrimp, peeled, deveined and washed**	**A few dashes black pepper**
1/2 **teaspoon salt**	**3 tablespoons all-purpose flour**
1 clove garlic, mashed	1/2 **shell of a well beaten egg (reserve the other half)**
2 tablespoons minced onion	**2 tablespoons milk (mixed with**
2 drops Tabasco sauce	**the egg)**
1 teaspoon salad oil	1/3 **cup cracker or bread crumbs**
1 tablespoon vinegar	

Season shrimp with salt, pepper, garlic, onion, Tabasco sauce, oil, and vinegar. Place in a covered dish, and keep in refrigerator, let steep in marinade a few hours.

When ready to fry, shake off loose seasoning. Using waxed paper to hold flour, coat each shrimp with flour, then with mixture of egg and milk, being careful not to soak too long. (Do this fast!)

Then Coat with cracker crumbs.

Fry in deep hot fat to a golden brown.

SHRIMP STEW À LA LOUISIANE

(2 Servings)

½ pound fresh shrimp, peeled,
  deveined, washed, and
  cut along the backs
1 teaspoon salt
¼ teaspoon red pepper
1 cup water
2 tablespoons cooking oil
3 tablespoons all-purpose flour

1 small onion, sliced fine
½ cup whole tomatoes, chopped
  (canned or fresh)
½ clove garlic, minced
½ cup water
A pinch nutmeg
2 hard-boiled eggs, peeled,
  and quartered

Boil shrimp in salted water 5 minutes; let cool in broth. Drain, reserve liquid; keep shrimp in covered dish until ready for use.

In a heavy-bottomed saucepan, heat oil; add flour; stir constantly until a golden brown; take pan away from heat for fear of burning. Add onion and garlic; cook 3 or 4 minutes, place over heat again. Add tomatoes, water, nutmeg, and shrimp broth; cook over medium heat about 15 minutes. Add shrimp and heat through. Salt and pepper again.

*FUN COOKING GUIDE: Serve on hot rice in a soup dish, garnish with eggs. Delicious served with a side dish of tossed salad. Can use oysters instead of shrimp to sauce.

MYRTLE'S CRAB MEAT AU GRATIN

1 lb. white crabmeat (remove
all bits of shell - I like to
boil crabs and pick out meat)
3 tablespoons butter or
  margarine
½ cup finely chopped onions or
  scallions
¼ cup finely chopped celery
1 heaping tablespoon all
  purpose flour
1½ cups milk
1 egg yolk, well beaten

½ teaspoon prepared mustard
¾ cup grated cheese (your choice
  cheddar or American)
  or dry white wine.
1 small pinch ground nutmeg
  "the ghost of a shadow"
white pepper, red hot pepper or
  cayenne to taste
3 tablespoons bread crumbs
¼ cup extra cheese
2 tablespoons fresh lemon juice
Dash of paprika

In a heavy saucepan, over moderate heat, melt butter; add onions and celery. Cook, stirring occasionally until onions are soft and transparent but not brown. Stir in the flour; blend well. Add milk, stir constantly until smooth. Add pepper, nutmeg, mustard, and cheese.

Take pot away from heat. Beat egg yolk and add lemon juice. Then add crabmeat - mix well. Butter a bake pan or individual bake dishes. Pour mixture, over all.

Combine cheese and bread crumbs, sprinkle over top of mixture, then add a dash of paprika. Bake 15 or 20 minutes until top is au gratin, brown and crusty.

*FUN COOKING GUIDE: For a different treat, can substitute with anchovies; Italian sausage; smoked sausage, boiled before using on pizza. Or one can use mushroom, or well-cooked seasoned ground beef.

TUNA AND GREEN BEAN CASSEROLE

1 can tuna fish
³/₄ cup boiled green beans
½ cup egg noodles
⅓ cup grated American cheese
4 tablespoons butter

2 tablespoons flour
1 small onion, cut fine
½ cup milk
Paprika

Preheat oven 350°F.

Cook onion in butter 2 or 3 minutes or until tender; add flour and blend well; add milk, stirring and cook until smooth; add cheese and cook until cheese melts. Set aside to cool. Season with salt and pepper.

Cook noodles according to directions on package; drain, then pour into a large bowl, add tuna, beans, and sauce; pour into a small greased baking dish, dust with paprika. Bake 25 minutes or until top is brown.

OYSTER STEW

(Serves 2)

1½ dozen oysters
2 tablespoons butter
2 tablespoons onion, chopped
1 tablespoon celery
2 tablespoon flour

2½ cups milk and oyster liquid
Salt and pepper to taste
1 tablespoon parsley, chopped
Dash of paprika
Dash of nutmeg

Sauté onion and celery in butter until soft; add flour and stir until smooth. Add milk; cook and stir until mixture boils.

Season to taste with salt and pepper. Add parsley, paprika, nutmeg, and oysters. Cook 2 minutes or until edges of oysters curl.

*FUN COOKING GUIDE: Never reheat oysters after cooked. If to be served later, do not add oysters, until just before ready to serve.

❖ *Chicken or Turkey* ❖

GREEN RICE MOLD WITH CHICKEN SUPREME
*My Third Award Winner

(Serves 6 to 8)

1-2½ to 3 pound fryer
A few chopped celery leaves
1 teaspoon salt
4 tablespoons cooking oil
4 tablespoons all purpose flour
2 tablespoons butter
1¾ cup chicken broth
¼ cup evaporated milk

1 medium onion, chopped fine
1-2 oz. can mushrooms
½ cup fresh frozen peas,
    boiled and drained
2 tablespoons pimiento,
    chopped
1 egg yolk

Place chicken, salt, celery leaves in a large pot with water to cover. Boil, then reduce heat and simmer, cover. Cook about 1½ hours or until just done. Do not overcook. Leave meat in stock until cool. Reserve 1¾ cups stock for sauce.

Debone chicken, leaving meat in large serving pieces.

Sauté mushrooms in butter. In a separate saucepan add flour to heated oil, stirring until light golden. Remove from heat, and sauté onions a bit; add stock and milk; stir until thick and smooth; season with salt to taste. Add beaten egg yolk, mushrooms, and chicken. Heat through.

GREEN RICE MOLD:

2 cups row rice
½ cup or 1 block butter or
    margarine
1 small onion, chopped fine

¼ cup chopped green onion tops
¼ cup chopped parsley
1 egg white, stiffly beaten
few dashes white pepper

Preheat oven 350°F.

Cook onion until tender in 2 tablespoons butter. Set aside. Cook rice according to directions on package. While still hot, stir in cooked onion

34

and remaining butter. Add pepper, parsley, green onion. Gently fold in the stiffly beaten egg white.

Grease a ring mold. Pack rice mixture into it; place mold in a larger pan of hot water. Cover top with foil, and bake 20 minutes. Run knife around mold, and invert on a platter.

When ready to serve, pour chicken supreme around rice mold and sprinkle peas and pimiento over all.

I garnished with carrot flowers and radish flowers for award.

*FUN COOKING GUIDE: This makes a nice company dish and will serve 6 or 8 people. Can be fixed ahead of time; if you decide to bake rice at the last moment, add beaten egg white only when ready to place in oven.

BAKED BREAST OF CHICKEN
(A Company Treat)

(6 Servings)

6 breasts of chicken	¼ teaspoon thyme
2 teaspoons salt	¼ teaspoon marjoram
¼ teaspoon red pepper	1 clove garlic, minced
¼ teaspoon basil	1 tablespoon apple cider vinegar
¼ teaspoon rosemary	2 tablespoons olive oil

In a bowl combine all the seasonings to make a marinade. Put chicken breasts in mixture and coat well. Cover dish and put in the refrigerator several hours, turning occasionally to coat. Reserve marinade.

Coat each breast with flour. In hot cooking fat fry each piece until brown, but not done. Place each piece, skin side up in a large piece of foil. Bring edges together and seal. Place in a shallow baking dish. Bake in a preheated oven, 350°F, 45 minutes. In meantime, make sauce.

SAUCE:

3 tablespoons cooking oil	¼ cup shallots or minced onion
3 tablespoons all purpose flour	¼ pound chicken livers
1½ cups water	¼ cup sherry wine
¼ cup butter	

In a saucepan, make a roux by adding flour to heated oil. Cook over medium heat, stirring constantly until a golden brown. Add water, stirring until sauce comes to a boil. Cook about 15 .minutes longer. Add seasoning from marinade.

In another saucepan cook livers and shallots in butter 8 or 10 minutes. Cool. Cut livers and shallots in very small pieces. Combine with sauce. Add wine.

After chicken breasts have cooked 45 minutes take out of oven and unwrap. Spoon liver sauce over meat and rewrap. Bake 15 minutes longer.

*FUN COOKING GUIDE: Be a guest at your own party. Many hours before serving, bake breasts of chicken, make sauce and chill until time for guests to arrive. Bake 20 minutes before serving time.

Bake them in one large piece of foil, then rewrap in individual foil with sauce added.

CHICKEN BROTH FOR GIBLET GRAVY AND CORN BREAD DRESSING

½ **pound chicken giblets**	1 **teaspoon salt**
1½ **pint water**	¼ **teaspoon cayenne**
¼ **cup chopped celery leaves**	**A small piece of bay leaf**

Put giblets, water, celery leaves, salt, cayenne, and bay leaf in a saucepan that covers; place over high heat when it comes to a boil, reduce to simmer; cover and cook 1½ hours or until tender. Set aside to cool.

Use for gravy and dressing.

*FUN COOKING GUIDE: For a more delicious broth, use bony parts and necks of chicken.

GIBLET GRAVY

(6 Servings)

½ **pound cooked giblets, finely diced**	**Half a clove of garlic, finely minced**
4 **chicken livers (optional)**	1½ **cup chicken broth**
3 **tablespoons butter or margarine**	1½ **teaspoon cornstarch, mixed with** ¼ **cup water**
1 **small onion, chopped fine**	**Salt and pepper to taste**

In a saucepan sauté onion and garlic until tender; add liver and cook 5 minutes; chop liver fine; set aside.

In a separate saucepan, heat broth over medium heat; mix cornstarch with water gradually; add to heated broth stirring until thick and smooth; then add giblet, liver and onion mixture. Heat and season to taste.

Serve over chicken or cornbread dressing.

CORN BREAD DRESSING

2 cups best ever corn bread,
  crumbled and firmly packed
  (see page 89)
2 slices very stale white bread
1-⅓ cup chicken broth
3 tablespoons butter
1 small onion, chopped fine
¼ cup chopped celery
¼ teaspoon thyme

¼ teaspoon oregano
¼ teaspoon cayenne
Salt to taste
1 well beaten egg, mixed with
  ¼ cup evaporated milk
1 tablespoon chopped green
  onion
1 tablespoon chopped parsley
paprika for topping

In a small saucepan sauté onion and celery in butter. Set aside.

In a large bowl combine corn bread, stale bread and cooled broth. Mix thoroughly, then add cooked onion and celery, egg and milk, thyme, oregano, cayenne, green onion and parsley. Mix well, pour into a well greased baking dish, dust top with paprika; cover with a lid; and bake in a 350° oven 45 minutes. Serve with giblet gravy.

LILY'S CORN BREAD DRESSING

½ pound cooked giblets,
  chopped
¼ pound chicken livers,
  chopped fine

1 tablespoon butter
All of the ingredients of the
  above cornbread dressing

Combine all in a mixing bowl, mix thoroughly; pour into a well-greased baking dish, bake in a 350° preheated oven 45 minutes. Serve with chicken or any kind of fowl.

*FUN COOKING GUIDE: Be a guest at your own party. Prepare corn bread mixture hours before serving time; then bake 1 hour.

CHICKEN FRICASSEE
(Louisiana version of chicken in brown gravy)

½ a fryer, cut in serving pieces
¼ cup cooking oil
¼ cup all-purpose flour
1 small onion, chopped fine
Small piece celery, chopped fine

Salt and pepper
¼ teaspoon thyme
1 clove garlic (optional)
1 pint water

Season meat with salt and pepper. Put in a covered dish and leave in this dish in the refrigerator for 2 or 3 hours.

In a large pot with a heavy bottom, heat oil. Add flour and cook over moderate heat, stirring constantly until golden brown. Take pot away from heat to keep from burning and add onion, celery, and garlic. Cook until tender, stirring 2 or 3 minutes. Add chicken and water. Cook over high heat. Stir constantly until mixture comes to a boil. Reduce heat to simmer. Cover pot with a lid and cook 1 hour. Add thyme and more water if sauce is too thick. Season to taste.

Serve with cooked rice or potatoes.

*FUN COOKING GUIDE: All the bony parts of a chicken can be used in the fricassee and the choice parts for frying later.

CHICKEN ÉTOUFFÉE

½ a fryer, cut in serving
  pieces
Salt and pepper
¼ cup oil

1 medium onion, finely
  chopped
Paprika

Season fryer generously with paprika, salt and pepper. Heat oil in heavy-bottomed pot with a lid. Fry the chicken to a golden brown, turning the pieces occasionally. When meat is brown cover with lid and reduce heat. Cook about 30 minutes, adding a tablespoon of water if necessary. Uncover and add onion. Cover and cook until tender, stirring occasionally. Serve with cooked rice.

CHICKEN HAWAIIAN

(4 Servings)

1 large frying chicken, cut in
 12 serving pieces
2 teaspoon salt
2 tablespoons cider vinegar
1 teaspoon sugar
⅛ teaspoon black pepper
2 tablespoons pineapple juice
1 tablespoon soy sauce
½ teaspoon ground ginger
 or mace
3 slices pineapple cut in
 12 pieces

3 tablespoons butter or
 margarine
⅓ cup flour
Cooking oil for frying 1 inch
 in depth
1 tablespoon cornstarch,
 mixed with ¼ cup water
1¼ cup pineapple juice with
 leftover marinade seasoning
paprika

Season chicken with next 7 ingredients. Place in a covered dish and chill in marinade several hours. Remove chicken from marinade. Reserve liquid and seasoning.

Coat each piece of chicken with flour and fry in hot fat to a golden brown, but not done. Remove each piece, placing skin side up in a greased baking dish that has a cover (or use foil). Place a piece of pineapple on each piece of chicken. Preheat oven 350°.

Pour out most of the oil in skillet leaving drippings. Add pineapple juice with marinade and cook over medium heat. Gradually add cornstarch with water and stir constantly until smooth and thick.

Add butter, salt, and pepper to taste. Spoon sauce over each piece of chicken and pineapple and dust with paprika. Cover and bake 40 minutes. Uncover and bake 15 or 20 minutes longer.

*FUN COOKING GUIDE: Be a guest at your own home! Prepare chicken long ahead of serving time, all ready for baking in a colorful baking dish.

FRIED CHICKEN

A small fryer, cut in serving
 pieces
Salt and pepper
½ cup all purpose flour

Depth of over an inch of
 cooking fat in frying pan
1 tablespoon water

About 2 hours or more before cooking time, season fryer with salt and pepper and put in a covered dish in the refrigerator.

Put flour in a small bag and coat each piece of chicken, one at a time. Heat fat. Put in the pieces of chicken; avoid crowding. Add 1 tablespoon of water and reduce heat. Quickly cover with a tight-fitting lid and let cook 10 minutes. Uncover, but do not touch it yet. Turn up the heat and fry to a golden brown, then gently turn over the pieces, being careful not to prick meat. Continue cooking until the chicken is brown and crispy. Take up each piece and add more pieces.

MILK GRAVY:

2 tablespoons all-purpose flour   **1¼ cups milk**

Drain off some of the fat, leaving about 2 tablespoons fat and drippings. Add flour and blend well. Add milk. Cook, stirring constantly until smooth, approximately 2 or 3 minutes. Season to taste.

*FUN COOKING GUIDE: The bony pieces of chicken can be used for gumbo, dumplings, fricassee, soup, stew, dressing, jambalaya, or smothered with onions and mushrooms.

CHICKEN JAMBALAYA

(4 to 6 Servings)

1 pound chicken, cut in small pieces (good way to use up bony parts)	**1 stick celery, chopped fine**
	1 cup raw rice
	2 cups water
2 tablespoons cooking oil	**¼ teaspoon thyme**
1 medium onion, cut in small pieces	**1 tablespoon chopped parsley**
	A very little chopped green onion

Season chicken with salt and pepper. Put oil and chicken in a large heavy-bottomed pan; cover with a lid, cook over medium heat for 20 minutes. Reduce heat and cook 10 minutes longer. Uncover and brown well; add onion and celery; cook about 10 minutes. Spoon out meat and most of the onion and celery into a dish and set aside. To the drippings, add rice and stir to coat well. Add water and ½ teaspoon salt. Cover and cook over low heat 20 minutes. Uncover and add cooked meat mixture and thyme; cook 15 minutes, stirring occasionally. Add parsley and green onion just before serving.

*FUN COOKING GUIDE: When the rice is put into the meat mixture raw, it is called jambalaya. When the rice is put in cooked, it is called dressing. Therefore, the above jambalaya can be made into dressing by mixing cooked rice into the cooked meat. This is according to French Creole custom.

SPECIAL SUNDAY CHICKEN
GIBLET DRESSING
(CAJUNS CALL THIS DIRTY RICE)

½ pound or 8-10 chicken giblets
2 cups water
¼ cup finely cut onion
(and this is Vitamin K)

¼ cup finely cut celery
½ teaspoon salt
¼ teaspoon cayenne

In a saucepan with a good cover add all the ingredients. Put over high heat. Reduce heat and simmer; and cook about two hours, or until meat is fork tender. Cool, cut meat into small pieces.

Then, make a Roux by using:

2 tablespoons cooking oil
1 tablespoon all-purpose flour
½ cup finely cut onion
About 2 cups cooked rice (See page 72 or 73)

1 or 2 fresh clove of garlic, minced
Cooked giblet and precious juice

Heat oil in a heavy-bottomed pot, add flour, cook slowly stirring constantly until color of an "Old Old Copper Penny", or color of "Melted Hershey Bar", pull pot away from heat, add onion, cook until tender. Add giblet and juices. Then add garlic. Cook until consistency of a thick gravy, stir in the rice. Season if needed with salt and cayenne. May add chopped green onion and parsley.

*FUN COOKING GUIDE: When purchasing whole chicken, the giblets included may be used for the chicken giblets in the ingredients above.

CHICKEN LIVERS DELUXE

½ pound chicken livers
½ teaspoon salt
¼ teaspoon red pepper
Pinch of chili powder
Pinch of thyme powder
1 teaspoon salad oil
1 tablespoon vinegar

½ teaspoon soy sauce
1 clove garlic, mashed
¼ cup all-purpose flour
3 tablespoons cooking oil
1 medium onion, chopped fine
1 small can mushrooms
1 tablespoon butter

Wash chicken livers in cold water. There should be no trace of gall. Drain well. Put into a bowl and add the next 8 ingredients. Let steep in this marinade an hour or longer.

Drain liver and reserve marinade. Coat each piece of liver with flour. Fry in heated oil, browning lightly. Remove to platter. To oil add onion and cook until tender. Add marinade and mushrooms and simmer 1 minute. Add liver and cover with a tight-fitting lid. Simmer 5 minutes longer. Add butter.

Serve with grits, mashed potatoes, cooked rice, or on toast.

*FUN COOKING GUIDE: For a more elegant dish, add ¼ cup sauterne wine instead of the marinade mixture to the onion.

BAKED TURKEY

No matter what size turkey you plan on cooking, directions will be on wrapper; BUT:

*FUN COOKING GUIDE: Wrap turkey giblets in a piece of aluminum foil and bake with the turkey; by all means bake breast down on a rack, in a large bake pan; then all the delicious juices from the back flows into the breast. When it is tender, turn the bird over and brown. Take out to serving platter, and make gravy. Delicious served over turkey or cornbread dressing.

TURKEY BONE BROTH

After turkey has been carved and served, slice or cut off ALL OF THE MEAT, wrap separately, then put turkey bones in plenty of water, and boil about an hour, or until remaining meat falls off the bones.

*FUN COOKING GUIDE: Discard the bone, freeze broth to be used later for turkey stew, soufflé, gravy, gumbo, or soup.

TURKEY GIBLET GRAVY

turkey giblets, chopped
turkey liver, chopped
1 small onion, chopped
dripping and juices from
    baked turkey

1½ cups water
1½ tablespoons cornstarch
    diluted in ¼ cup water

There should be juices in the pan, place pan on top of the stove, add onion, cook until tender, add cooked giblets, water, and boil. Blend cornstarch in water. Add to giblet gravy; stir and cook about 15 minutes.

CHICKEN OKRA GUMBO

2½ to 3 pound fryer cut in
  serving pieces
1/3 cup cooking fat
½ cup all purpose flour
1 medium onion chopped fine
2 quarts water
1 pound okra fresh or frozen,
  sliced thin

1 cup canned whole tomatoes;
  cut small
2 cloves garlic minced fine
a small stick celery chopped tine
a small bay leaf, optional
salt and red pepper to taste

Season meat with salt and pepper. In a heavy-bottomed pot, heat fat; add flour, stir constantly until a dark golden brown, add onion cook about 5 minutes. Add chicken, water, garlic celery, bay leaf, and tomatoes. When liquid comes to a hard boil, add okra. When it boils again reduce heat to simmer, season again with salt and pepper to taste. Cook about 1½ hour. Serve hot, in soup bowls with rice.

*FUN COOKING GUIDE: For a different taste treat, sausage or oysters may be added.

❖ Beef ❖

PAPA'S $1,000,000.00 BAR-B-Q SAUCE
That was the start of a Restaurant Chain

1 lb. ground chuck - doesn't matter if it is fat, good for daubing
½ cup cooking oil
¼ cup all purpose flour
2 cups chopped onion
1 cup chopped celery "leaves are fine"
2½ pints water
1 teaspoon prepared mustard

2 tablespoon Worcestershire Sauce
2 cloves garlic, minced
1 thin slice lemon
½ cup catsup for spicy flavor
2 6 oz. cans tomato paste "not the sauce"
2 teaspoons salt
½ teaspoon red pepper
2 tablespoons butter

Make a roux by heating oil, add flour, cook over medium heat, stir constantly until dark brown; add onion, take pot away from heat for fear of burning. Stir, cook until tender about 10 minutes. Add meat, celery, water, mustard, Worcestershire Sauce, garlic, lemon, catsup, tomato paste, salt, and pepper. Stir, simmer, cook about 1½ to 2 hours. Add butter.

Add 1 or 2 drops of smoke liquid, can be bought in grocery stores, or optional.

When sauce cools, oil emerges to the top; Papa used this oil to daubed meat; when grill Bar-B-Q-ing. And bottom meat sauce served with Italian or French bread; along with the meat.

PAPA'S BAR-B-Q'D RIBS

Whatever amount of Pork ribs used, Papa always parboiled the well seasoned pork with just a little amount of water, chopped celery and onion, cover and cook until just tender; then put meat on the grill to Bar-B-Q with oil coating. Turn meat only once. Juices from the parboiled meat may be used for jambalaya on page 35.

PAPA'S BAR-B-Q'D PORK SAUSAGE

Boil sausage a little while before putting on grill. Never prick with a fork; for fear of losing precious juices. Daubed sausage with Papa's Bar-B-Q sauce.

PAPA'S BAR-B-Q'D
CHICKEN, BEEF, LAMB

Papa grilled any; with Bar-B-Q sauce oil. Served meat sauce along.

*FUN COOKING GUIDE - sauce may be used with:
   Boiled crabs - Boil crabs, then marinate - pour Bar-B-Q sauce over crabs then oven Bar-B-Q for 20 minutes.
   Any meat or fish - Baked with the sauce.
   Baked Macaroni and Cheese - served with the sauce.
   Spaghetti - with sauce.
   Baked eggplant casserole.
   Hamburgers - served with sauce.
   Wieners - served with sauce.

*FUN COOKING GUIDE: Make more sauce than needed, then freeze in small plastic containers for future use.

BEEFBURGER CHEESE FILLING:

½ pound ground beef
1 onion, chopped fine
½ cup dry bread crumbs
Half egg shell of beaten egg
¼ cup milk
1 tablespoon Worcestershire
   sauce

1 tablespoon Catsup
¼ teaspoon prepared mustard
Salt and cayenne to taste
3 slice yellow cheese cut in
   smaller slices

Preheat oven 450°. Combine all ingredients except cheese, mix well, arrange on pie shell, bake 10 minutes; reduce heat to 350°, bake about 25 minutes longer. Take from oven and place sliced cheese over all; return to oven, and bake only until cheese melts.

*FUN COOKING GUIDE: Can prepare pie and meat filling hours before baking but do not add meat to pie until ready to bake.

BEEF AND MACARONI MEXICANA
(2 Servings)

½ pound ground meat
1½ cups macaroni (break in
   small pieces; cook in ample
   salted water 20 minutes;
   drain; rinse with warm
   water once)
2 tablespoon olive oil or
   cooking fat
1 medium onion, chopped fine
1 cup water

1 stick celery, chopped fine
1 green pepper, cut in
   small pieces
1 small can whole tomatoes
2 tablespoons Italian
   tomato paste
1 clove garlic, minced
1 bay leaf
½ teaspoon chili powder

Use a heavy skillet with a tight-fitting lid. Brown meat in heated oil, stirring occasionally. Add onion, and cook 2 or 3 minutes. Add water, tomatoes, celery, green pepper and garlic. Cook 30 minutes over low heat. Add bay leaf, chili powder, macaroni, salt and pepper to taste. Cook a while longer and if water is needed, add.

*FUN COOKING GUIDE: Also try substituting spaghetti.

BONELESS BIRDS
(4 Servings)

1 pound round steak (cut in
   4 equal portions ½" thick)
2 slices breakfast bacon
   chopped in small pieces
1 medium onion, chopped fine
2 cloves garlic, mashed

¼ cup all-purpose flour
2 tablespoons cooking oil
Pinch marjoram powder
Salt and pepper to taste
4 or more toothpicks

Pound the edges of meat with a meat pounder or edge of a saucer.

Season with salt and pepper. Combine bacon, onion, and garlic; place one tablespoon of this mixture in center of each piece of steak. Fold each and fasten edges securely with two toothpicks. Coat these with flour. Heat oil in skillet and brown meat on all sides. Add the remaining bacon and onion mixture with 1 cup water. Cover with a tight-fitting lid and simmer over very low fire one hour, stirring occasionally. Add more water when and if necessary. Add marjoram powder and cook 15 minutes longer.

*FUN COOKING GUIDE: The pieces of meat will shape up during the process of cooking to look like birds. You will find the gravy delicious served with creamed potatoes or cooked rice.

HOT TAMALE PIE

(4 Servings)

Filling for dough

½ cup corn meal (preferably the yellow)
1 cup beef broth; canned or can make with bouillon cube
2 tablespoons tomato sauce
1 cup water

½ teaspoon salt
2 teaspoons chill powder
¼ teaspoon garlic powder
¼ teaspoon red pepper
2 tablespoons cooking fat
½ teaspoon sugar

In a bowl combine cornmeal, salt, chili powder, garlic powder, sugar, and water, mix until thoroughly blended.

In a saucepan heat broth with cooking fat to boiling, gradually add corn meal mixture, stirring constantly, reduce heat to low and cook 20 minutes. Stir occasionally.

Pour cooked mixture into a shallow baking dish; when it has cooled enough to congeal, add chili con carne.

*FUN COOKING GUIDE: Be a guest, line a bake pan with a large piece of aluminum foil, pour the mixture, and chill or freeze the hot tamale pie, for later use.

*FUN COOKING GUIDE: I like making my own beef broth. Ask butcher to give or sell some beef bones. In a large kettle add water, bones, salt, pepper, onion, celery, tomato sauce and chili powder. Over medium heat, cook for 1 or 2 hours. Strain, measure, and use in above pie. Make more tamale pie and freeze, very economical.

CHILI CON CARNE

2 tablespoons cooking fat
½ pound ground beef
1 medium onion chopped
1 cup whole tomatoes, chopped
1 tablespoon tomato sauce
⅛ teaspoon red pepper

Small piece bay leaf
Half clove garlic
Salt to taste
½ cup cooked red kidney beans
1 teaspoon chili powder

In a saucepan, combine meat, cooking fat, onion, garlic, salt, chili powder and red pepper cook over medium heat, and brown lightly, stirring occasionally. Add tomatoes, bay leaf and 1 cup water, when it comes to a hard boil, reduce heat to simmer, and cook 45 minutes; add beans and more water if mixture gets too thick, cook 15 minutes longer. Cool.

Pour mixture over cooked corn meal, sprinkle with a small bag of Fritos or other cornchips, grate yellow cheese over top; then bake in a moderate oven about 15 minutes.

HAMBURGER PATTIES

(2 Servings)

½ pound ground lean beef
1 small onion, chopped
1 tablespoon butter
½ slice stale bread, soaked in
4 tablespoons milk
½ beaten egg (reserve the other half for other use)

½ teaspoon salt
1 teaspoon of egg to coat patties
Half a clove of garlic, minced
Bit of cayenne or red pepper
1 tablespoon cooking oil

Sauté onion in butter until golden. Combine egg and bread mixture. Add mixture to meat, onions, and seasoning. Mix well and divide into 4 equal parts. Flatten and shape oblong; coat each with egg. Heat cooking oil in a heavy iron skillet and fry the patties on each side 6 or 8 minutes.

*FUN COOKING GUIDE: This same meat mixture is fine for spaghetti and meat ball dish. Shape meat into round balls instead of patties. Make your favorite tomato sauce and add meat balls, cook about 30 minutes for spaghetti dish,

MEATBALL SURPRISE WITH GRAVY

(2 Servings)

¾ pound ground beef
½ shell of egg, well beaten,
   (reserve 1 tablespoon egg
   to coat meatballs)
2 tablespoons milk
¼ cup bread crumbs
6 prunes, pitted
6 pieces apple or pineapple

3 tablespoons cooking oil
1½ tablespoons all-purpose flour
1 small onion, chopped
1¼ cups water
1 small can mushrooms
   (optional)
Pinch nutmeg

Stuff each prune with a piece of apple or pineapple. Set aside. Combine meat, egg, milk, bread crumbs, salt and pepper to taste. Mix well. Divide into 6 equal portions and in center of each place a stuffed prune. Shape into a round ball. Coat with egg. Brown in heated oil, but do not cook until done. Remove to platter. Add flour to oil, stirring constantly. Cook to a golden brown, take pot off the heat for fear of burning. Add onion, cook 3 or 4 minutes. Add meat balls, mushrooms, water and nutmeg. Cook over medium heat 20 minutes. Season with salt and pepper to taste and cook ten minutes longer, adding water to sauce if necessary. Serve with creamed potatoes, rice or grits.

OLIVE-BURGER PIE

(4 Servings)

Biscuit or pie dough - enough
   to cover bottom of pie pan
¾ pound ground beef
1 tablespoon bacon drippings
1 medium onion, chopped
½ cup tomato sauce
½ teaspoon sugar
½ teaspoon chili powder

1 small clove garlic, mashed
   (if desired)
¼ teaspoon oregano powder
½ cup ripe olives, chopped
Salt and pepper to taste
1 fresh tomato, sliced
½ cup American cheese, grated

Cook meat in drippings until done (about 20 minutes). Add water and stir occasionally. Add onion and cook 5 minutes, stirring constantly. Add tomato sauce, water, garlic, chili powder, sugar and oregano. Simmer about 25 minutes. Set aside to cool. When cool add olives.

Roll out dough. Place on pie pan and flute edges. Pour mixture of meat into pie pan. Top with sliced tomato and sprinkle with grated cheese. Bake 15 to 18 minutes in 350° preheated oven.

*FUN COOKING GUIDE: The sauce can be made ahead of time and chilled until ready to bake in pie crust or biscuit dough.

ROAST BEEF SUPREME

One 2-pound roast (a "seven" or any shoulder cut is suggested)	1 clove garlic
	2 tablespoons flour
	Salt and pepper to taste
1 tablespoon prepared mustard	2 tablespoons cooking oil

Make small slits with a sharp knife and insert slivers of garlic. Season meat with salt and red pepper; rub mustard into meat well and coat with flour. Preheat cooking oil in Dutch oven or heavy iron pot until piping hot. Place meat in pot and brown on all sides. Turn heat very low and cook about 1½ hours or until tender. A little water may be added if and when needed. Do not prick with fork or pointed object when turning, for you will lose most of the precious juices. Take roast up on warm platter and keep warm until served.

GRAVY

To the drippings and fat from the roast add one small onion, chopped fine; cook until tender, then add one cup of water. When this starts boiling, dissolve 1 tablespoon cornstarch in ¼ cup water and add to boiling mixture. Stir until it thickens. This makes a delicious brown gravy.

STEAK À LA SAUCE (ROUILLE)

(4 Servings)

1 pound tender beef steak, cut
   ½ inch thick
Salt
Red pepper

¼ cup cooking oil
1 medium onion, sliced fine
Water

Season steak with salt and pepper. In a heavy-bottomed skillet, put meat in cold oil. Over medium heat, cook until most of the liquid has cooked out. Turn meat, and add 1 tablespoon water, cook until meat starts frying, then turn meat and add water. Continue with the process of turning, frying, and adding water until meat is tender, then add onion, cook until tender, add a little water. This makes a sauce rouille, or rusty gravy. Serve with cooked rice or creamed potatoes.

*FUN COOKING GUIDE: The idea of using cold fat to start cooking steak or any meat will tenderize meat.

SWEDISH MEATBALLS

(4 to 6 Servings)

1½ cups ground beef
½ cups ground pork
3 tablespoons bread crumbs,
   mixed with ½ shell of
   beaten egg, and
   2 tablespoons evaporated milk
1 small onion, finely minced,
   cooked in
   1 tablespoon butter

2 dashes nutmeg
2 teaspoon salt
Cayenne to taste
1 small onion, chopped fine
½ cup tomato sauce
1 cup water
1 teaspoon beaten egg to coat
   meat before frying
½ inch cooking oil in skillet

Combine bread and egg mixture and cooked onion with meat. Season with salt, cayenne, and nutmeg. Mix well. Shape into very small balls the size of a walnut. Coat with beaten egg. Fry in oil until brown. Shake pan while browning to turn them over. Remove to a dish.

Cook onion in the drippings until tender, stirring constantly. Add tomato sauce, water and cooked meat. Cover with a lid. Cook about 20 minutes over low heat. Add ¼ teaspoon sugar to sauce.

*FUN COOKING GUIDE: These meatballs can be made the size of marbles, fry rolling around in the frying pan, take out, make sauce, then add meatballs to sauce. Serve as a cocktail snack or as an hors d'oeuvre.

SWISS STEAK

1 pound round steak, cut
2 inches thick
1 medium onion, sliced thin
Salt and pepper to taste
(red pepper preferred)
1 tablespoon Worcestershire
sauce
1 clove garlic, minced
¼ teaspoon sugar

1 small piece green pepper,
chopped fine
1 cup whole tomatoes (canned
or fresh ripe) cut in small
pieces
2 tablespoons shortening
3 tablespoons flour
1¼ cup sherry wine (optional)

Season steak well with salt and pepper. Pound flour into the meat with tenderizer mallet or edge of saucer. Heat shortening in a heavy iron skillet, and brown meat on both sides. Add onion and cook 2 or 3 more minutes. Add tomatoes, sugar, garlic and ½ cup water. Let simmer for about 2 hours, or until meat is completely tender. Add more water if necessary. Add green pepper and Worcestershire sauce and simmer for 15 minutes. If sherry wine is used, add just before removing from fire.

*FUN COOKING GUIDE: Delicious served with hot rice.

FRIED VEAL CUTLETS

(2 Servings)

½ pound veal cutlets, cut
½ inch thick
1 tablespoon vinegar

Salt and pepper to taste
¼ cup flour
Water

Season meat with salt, pepper, and vinegar; put in a covered dish and chill many hours before cooking.

Coat each piece of meat with flour.

Heat cooking oil over high heat in a heavy-bottomed skillet, about 1 inch in depth. Add meat and 1 tablespoon water, reduce heat to low; cover with a tight-fitting lid; cook about 10 minutes. Uncover; raise heat to medium, but do not disturb meat; brown, turn meat (do not cover again); and brown. Take up on platter. Make cream gravy with the drippings.

CREAM GRAVY

1½ tablespoons drippings
1½ tablespoons flour

1¼ cup milk
Salt and pepper

Add flour to drippings, blend well; add milk; cook and stir constantly until thick and smooth. Salt and pepper to taste.

*FUN COOKING GUIDE: This dish is good served with boiled potatoes.

SWEETBREAD SUPREME
(A Meat Delicacy)

2 pairs sweetbread
2 tablespoons butter, melted
2 tablespoons flour

Salt and pepper
Paprika

Clean and soak sweetbread in cold water one hour. Plunge them into salted boiling water and cook gently 20 minutes. Take them out of hot water and place in cold water 5 minutes. They will become firm again. Drain sweetbread and season with salt, red pepper, and paprika. Coat them with flour. Cook in butter, browning both sides. Serve hot.

*FUN COOKING GUIDE: The sweetbread can be prepared long in advance, then sautéed in butter moments before serving. And for a different taste treat add ¼ cup sherry.

VEAL LIVER AND ONIONS

4 serving pieces of veal liver,
    cut ½ inch thick
Salt and pepper

1 large onion, sliced thin
¼ cup cooking oil
¼ cup flour

Season liver and coat with flour. Heat oil in skillet over medium heat. Fry liver brown on each side. Should take 5 minutes. Place liver on platter and keep warm. Fry onions in the drippings, stirring constantly; return liver to skillet and cover with a tight-fitting lid. Cook 5 minutes longer. Do not overcook, as it will toughen. Serve with grits or cooked rice.

*FUN COOKING GUIDE: To save time and money, prepare the liver with seasoning and flour, wrap in freezer paper, chill and freeze. When ready to use, do not defrost but add to hot fat and cook a little longer.

BEEF OKRA GUMBO

2 pound stewing beef or
  brisket
⅓ cup cooking oil
½ cup all purpose flour
1 medium onion chopped
2 quarts water
1 stick celery chopped to make
½ cup

1 clove garlic minced
1 cup whole canned tomatoes
  cut in pieces
1 pound okra fresh or frozen,
  sliced thin
salt and red pepper to taste
1 small piece bay leaf.

Season meat with salt and pepper then set aside. In a heavy-bottomed pot, heat oil, add flour, stir constantly until dark golden brown, add onions and meat. Reduce heat to low; cover, stirring occasionally, and cook about 20 minutes. Raise heat, add water, garlic, celery and bay leaf, cook about 30 minutes. Add to gumbo, the tomatoes and okra, cook about 1 hour longer or until meat is tender. If gumbo liquid reduced too much, add water, serve in soup plates with rice.

❖ Pork, Lamb, Ham, ❖
Sauces for Ham

PORK AND GIBLET JAMBALAYA
(My Third Award at International Rice Festival)

(6 Servings)

3 tablespoons cooking oil
1 pound lean pork, cut in
   1-inch pieces
½ pound chicken, giblets
1 teaspoon salt
¼ teaspoon, red pepper
1½ cups raw rice
3 cups water
1 medium onion, chopped
1 stick celery, chopped

1 cup whole tomatoes, chopped;
1 clove garlic, mashed
2 tablespoons butter
¼ teaspoon thyme
¼ teaspoon oregano
2 tablespoons green onion,
   chopped.
2 tablespoons parsley, chopped
¼ cup sherry wine (Optional)

In a large pot with a heavy bottom, combine pork, giblets, oil, salt and red pepper; cover with a tight-fitting lid, cook over medium heat 1½ to 2 hours or until tender, stirring and adding water frequently. Then add onion, garlic, and celery; cook about 5 minutes. Dish out: meat and seasoning, reserve oil and drippings. Cut meat in small pieces. Set aside.

To oil and drippings, add tomatoes, cook about 5 minutes; add rice and coat well, stirring. Then add water, and when the mixture comes to a boil, reduce the heat, cover with a tight-fitting lid, and cook about 25 minutes. Then add cooked meat mixture, butter thyme and oregano. Cook 20 minutes longer; can stay covered till ready to serve, then add green onion, parsley, and wine. Serve hot.

*FUN COOKING GUIDE: This pork and giblet jambalaya can be served as a main dish; it is rich enough.

Pork and chicken dressing can be made with all the ingredients used in jambalaya, only omit water and raw rice, but use about 3 or 4 cups of cooked rice; make as above.

Serve with fried apple rings.

FRIED APPLE RINGS

1 medium apple, peeled and sliced ¼ inches thick Milk	flour 2 or 3 tablespoons melted butter

Dip apple rings in milk and coat with flour. Fry in 2 or 3 tablespoons melted butter until golden brown. Sprinkle with sugar (powdered or granulated). Serve hot, with ham or pork.

ALZACE'S PORK AND TURNIP STEW

(4 Servings)

1 pound lean pork, cut in 1-inch cubes	¼ teaspoon rosemary leaves
1½ tablespoons cooking oil or fat	salt and red pepper to taste
2 tablespoons all-purpose flour	turnips, peeled and diced to make about 2 cups
1 medium onion, finely chopped	1 tablespoon sugar
1 clove garlic, minced	1 pint water

Season pork with salt and pepper, let stand a while. Boil turnips in water with sugar added; cook about 15 minutes or until just tender. Drain; set aside.

In a large heavy bottom pot, heat the cooking oil. Add flour, stirring constantly until golden brown. Remove pot from heat for fear of burning. Add onion and garlic. Cook about 5 minutes, stirring constantly. Add pork and 2 cups water and stir until sauce begins to boil. Cover with a tight-fitting lid and reduce heat. Simmer 45 minutes to 1 hour, or until meat is tender. Add turnips, rosemary leaves, salt and pepper to taste. Cook about 10 minutes longer. Serve with hot cooked rice.

*FUN COOKING GUIDE: Boneless beef can be used instead of pork.

OVEN BAR-B-Q'D PORK RIBS

(4 Servings)

3 pounds pork ribs   **salt and pepper**
4 tablespoons cooking oil

Season ribs generously with salt and red pepper. In a large heavy-bottomed pot put ribs, oil, and 2 cups water. Cover with a tight-fitting lid and cook over medium heat. When this starts to boil, reduce heat, and simmer about 2 hours or until just tender. Stir and add water occasionally, if needed. Remove ribs and arrange on a shallow baking dish, meaty side down. Reserve drippings.

*FUN COOKING GUIDE: Drippings make a tasty jambalaya.

BAR-B-Q SAUCE GLAZE

¼ cup oil and drippings from   **1 teaspoon chili powder**
     cooked pork   **1 teaspoon Worcestershire sauce**
1 tablespoon minced onion   **1 tablespoon vinegar**
1 tablespoon prepared mustard   **¼ teaspoon paprika**
1 tablespoon brown sugar   **2 drops Bar-B-Q liquid smoke**
2 tablespoons catsup   **(available in store)**
1 tablespoon flour

Combine all eleven ingredients and mix well. Spread over bony side of meat. Bake in moderate oven about 15 minutes. Turn pork to meat side and brush sauce over all. Place pan under broiler about 6 inches from heat and glaze. Serve hot or cold.

*FUN COOKING GUIDE: May use beef brisket also. If you are having an outside Bar-B-Q; cook meat in advance but not too well done and chill until time to Bar-B-Q.

Pork rib drippings may be used for rice dressing or jambalaya.

PORK POT ROAST

2½ or 3 pound pork shoulder   **4 tablespoons cooking oil**
     roast   **salt and red pepper to taste**
1 tablespoon prepared mustard   **1 clove garlic, chopped**
¼ cup all-purpose flour   **(optional)**

One or two hours before cooking the roast, season generously with salt and pepper. Insert slivers of garlic in slits in roast made with a sharp knife.

Rub mustard all over the meat. Wrap well in foil and place in refrigerator until ready to cook.

When ready to cook, coat all sides with flour. Heat cooking oil in a large pot and cook meat to a golden brown on all sides. Cover pot with a tight-fitting lid; turn heat low and cook about 2 hours. If heat is low enough you should not have to add any water, but turn meat frequently, careful not to prick with a sharp object for fear of losing the precious juices.

MAKE THE DELICIOUS GRAVY AS FOLLOWS:

fat from the meat and pan drippings	1½ cups water
1 medium onion, grated	1 heaping tablespoon cornstarch with ¼ cup water
1 small piece of celery, chopped	

Cook onion and celery in meat drippings until clear and tender, stirring occasionally. Add water. When liquid comes to a boil, add cornstarch mixture. Cook until thick and smooth. Add more seasoning (salt and pepper) if necessary.

PORK CHOPS AND BEAN BAKE

(2 Servings)

2 or 4 pork chops ½ inch thick (shoulder, loin or rib)	2 tablespoons catsup
3 tablespoons cooking oil	1 teaspoon prepared mustard
1 can pork and beans	dash of nutmeg and cinnamon
1 small onion, chopped	⅓ cup corn flakes, crushed
2 tablespoons brown sugar	2 slices bacon, cut in small pieces

Preheat oven 325° F.

Season pork chops with salt and pepper. Heat oil in skillet and brown pork chops on both sides. In a large bowl combine beans, sugar, onion, catsup, mustard, and MIX WELL. Pour half the mixture in a greased baking dish. Place pork chops over it and then add remaining mixture. Sprinkle top with cornflakes and then with bacon. Bake 45 minutes uncovered.

PORK CHOPS IN MUSHROOM SAUCE

(2 Servings)

4 pork chops, cut ½ inch thick
3 tablespoons cooking oil
1 small onion, chopped
½ can Cream of Mushroom
   soup, mixed with
   2 cups water

1 teaspoon Worchestershire
   sauce
salt and red pepper
all-purpose flour

Season chops with salt and pepper. Coat well with flour. In a skillet heat oil and brown chops on both sides. Take up on platter. Cook onion in drippings until tender. Add mushroom soup and

water. When this comes to a boil add pork chops. Cover and reduce heat. Simmer 1 hour. Season to taste with salt, pepper, and Worcestershire sauce. Serve with cooked rice or mashed potatoes.

*FUN COOKING GUIDE: Taste. Salt may not be needed.

PORK CHOPS MIT APFEL IN SAUCE

2 double pork chops (ask
   butcher to make pocket
   in each)
4 thin slices of cooking apples
3 tablespoons cooking oil
1 cup whole tomatoes, chopped
   (canned or fresh)

1 cup water
1 small onion, chopped
1 clove garlic, minced (optional)
salt and pepper to taste
sprig of parsley, chopped
½ teaspoon sugar
1 teaspoon flour

Fill the slit in the chops with 2 slices each of apple. Secure with toothpicks. Season pork chops with salt and pepper.

Heat oil in heavy skillet. Add chops and cover with a tight-fitting lid.

Cook over medium heat about 45 minutes, occasionally adding water. Uncover and fry brown.

A few minutes before the chops are done pour off about 2 tablespoons fat into a saucepan. In the fat, sauté onion. Add tomatoes, garlic, water, salt, pepper and sugar. Simmer 10 or 15 minutes.

Dilute flour in a little water and stir into sauce.

Remove chops to platter and pour tomato sauce around chops. Garnish with sprigs of parsley.

GLAZED PORK CHOPS

2 pork chops, ½ inch thick   2 tablespoons apple jelly
  (shoulder or loin)   pinch of cinnamon
½ teaspoon salt   pinch of cloves
pepper   2 sprigs of parsley (optional)
2 tablespoons cooking oil

Season chops with salt and pepper. Heat oil in a heavy skillet, brown chops on each side. Cover with a lid and cook over low heat. Add water occasionally. Cook 25 or 30 minutes. Remove chops to a baking dish.

Mix together jelly and spices. Spread mixture over chops and place under broiler until thoroughly glazed. Garnish with sprigs of parsley.

Serve pan juices over creamed potatoes.

CREOLE SAUSAGE JAMBALAYA

(4 Servings)

½ pound pork sausage   1 clove garlic, mashed
1 cup raw rice   dash thyme (omit if sausage
1 tablespoon fat   is spicy)
1 medium onion, chopped   1½ tablespoons chopped parsley
1 small bell pepper, chopped   1½ tablespoons chopped green
1 stick celery, chopped   onion
1 small can whole tomatoes

Preheat fat in iron skillet or Dutch oven; add 1 cup water and crumbled sausage. Cook slowly until brown, stirring occasionally. Add onion, celery, tomatoes, bell pepper and garlic. Cook 5 minutes. Add rice and 1½ cups water, cook covered over very low heat 30 minutes or until water has cooked out. Stir occasionally. Add thyme, parsley and onion. Stir mixture well.

FUN COOKING GUIDE: Serve as a main dish with a green vegetable and I'd suggest you add to menu a pineapple salad or apple salad on a crisp lettuce leaf.

Pork ribs is also a delicious taste treat fixed in this manner, only cook pork a little longer.

COUNTRY STYLE SAUSAGE AND
BROWN GRAVY

(2 Servings)

¾ pound pork sausage in casing
1 tablespoon cooking oil
1 small onion, minced

1 clove garlic, minced
1 tablespoon cornstarch,
    dissolved in ¼ cup water

Put sausage, oil and 1½ cups water into a sauce pot. Over medium heat, bring to boil. Cover and reduce heat. Simmer 30 minutes. Uncover, add onion and garlic and cook 2 or 3 minutes. If all the water has cooked out, add 1 cup water. When sauce comes to a rolling boil, add cornstarch mixed with water. Cook over medium heat, stirring until sauce thickens and boils.

*FUN COOKING GUIDE: Very good served with rice or creamed potatoes.

SAUSAGE À-LA-CREOLE

(2 Servings)

½ pound link sausage, pork
1 cup water
1 cup whole canned tomatoes
2 tablespoons tomato paste
1 small onion, chopped fine
1 tablespoon celery leaves

a small piece of bay leaf
a pinch rosemary leaves
½ clove garlic, mashed
    a small piece green pepper,
    minced
½ teaspoon sugar

Place sausage and water in a skillet; cover and boil 20 minutes over medium heat. Uncover and let water cook out. Fry to a golden brown, using tongs to turn links. (Do not prick with fork or other sharp instrument, as this will cause meat to be dry and lose juices). Add onion and cook for 1 or 2 minutes. Add all remaining ingredients. Cover and simmer 30 minutes, stirring occasionally.

*FUN COOKING GUIDE: Serve with grits or mashed potatoes.

MOM'S SKILLET SAUSAGE IN WHITE WINE

¾ pound sausage (try to get
pork and beef mixed or
pure pork)
¼ cup white wine
1 medium onion, chopped

½ cup carrots, cooked in
boiling water until tender
(½ cup water)
salt and pepper

Place sausage with 1 cup water in a heavy skillet. Cook until all water is cooked out. Let it fry brown on both sides. Be careful not to prick or break, lest you lose the precious juices. Add onion. Cook until tender. Add 1/2 cup water and carrots. Boil 10 minutes. Add wine just before serving.

LAMB À LA LOUISIANE

(4 Servings)

1 pound lamb (breast or
    shoulder) cut in serving
    sizes or in 2" cubes
flour
salt
cayenne
1½ tablespoons cooking oil
4 small potatoes
1 cup tomato sauce
½ cup whole tomatoes, canned
    (or use an overripe tomato,
    cut in small pieces)

4 small onions, whole
1 small onion, chopped fine
1 small bay leaf
1 clove garlic
1 or 2 carrots cut in large pieces
dash of nutmeg
pinch of rosemary leaves
    (optional)
½ cup white wine (optional)

Salt and pepper each piece of meat and coat with flour. Brown pieces of lamb in hot cooking oil in Dutch oven. Add chopped onion and cook a while. Add tomatoes and water to cover meat

Simmer over low fire 1 hour or until tender. Add all remaining ingredients, except wine and nutmeg, and cook 30 minutes longer. Add wine and nutmeg just before serving. Serve piping hot.

*FUN COOKING GUIDE: Other vegetables, such as green peas, string beans and especially leftover vegetables, may be added.

LAMB PATTIES

½ pound ground lamb
4 strips breakfast bacon
½ teaspoon salt
⅛ teaspoon cayenne
dash fresh ground black pepper
dash nutmeg

⅛ teaspoon garlic powder
(optional)
2 tablespoons beaten egg
(refrigerate the other part
of egg for other uses)
2 tablespoon cooking oil

Combine all the ingredients except the bacon and oil. Form into four equal patties, and flatten. Wrap bacon around the edge and secure with a toothpick. Heat oil in a heavy skillet. Brown patties on each side, 8 or 10 minutes, turning only once. Use your egg spatula. Do not prick into meat so as not to lose the precious juices.

*FUN COOKING GUIDE: These patties can be bought from your butcher already made up, but they are not seasoned. Also, they are less expensive if you prepare them yourself.

TANTALIZING HAM LOAF

2 slices pineapple, broken in
chunks
2 cups cooked ham ground
1 cup fresh ground pork
or beef)
1 pinch of nutmeg
1 small onion, chopped
½ cup cracker crumbs, soaked
in ½ cup milk

2 tablespoons pineapple syrup
½ teaspoon brown sugar
1 tablespoon butter, melted
1 pinch of cinnamon
1 pinch of cloves
1 egg, beaten
½ teaspoon dry mustard
salt and pepper to taste

Preheat oven 350° F.

Grease a small deep baking dish. Mix pineapple syrup, butter, sugar and spices in a cup. Arrange pineapple chunks on bottom of baking dish and pour mixture over chunks. In a separate bowl combine ham, pork, onion, egg, mustard, crackers and milk. Season with salt and pepper. Spoon mixture into baking dish over pineapple chunks and spice sauce. Place dish in a pan of warm water and cover. Bake 30 minutes. Uncover and bake 15 minutes longer. To unmold, loosen meat from sides of dish and invert on a warm platter and remove baking dish. Very pretty and tasty.

*FUN COOKING GUIDE: This ham loaf may be served hot or cold or sliced for sandwiches.

BAKED HAM AND LIMA BEAN FLAMBÉ

(6 to 8 Servings)

½ pound large dried lima beans
2 cups diced, cooked ham
3 tablespoons bacon drippings
1 medium onion, chopped
1½ teaspoon salt
1 teaspoon sugar
1 clove garlic, minced
few dashes Tabasco sauce
jigger of rum

4 slices pineapple, each cut
  in half
1 extra slice pineapple
9 maraschino cherries
⅓ cup blanched almonds
1 tablespoon butter
1 teaspoon sugar
few dashes nutmeg

Wash beans and soak overnight or for several hours; cook beans in plenty of water. Add sugar, onion and salt. When they come to a hard boil, reduce heat to simmer, cover and cook about 2 hours or until beans are soft, but do not mash. Add Tabasco sauce and garlic during the cooking process. Mash ½ cup beans to thicken. Add ham to beans.

Pour into a large 1½ quart baking dish. Preheat oven 350° F. Arrange 8 pineapple halves around top of the beans, and the extra one in the center; place a cherry in each.

Combine butter, almonds, and sugar in a saucepan; heat through. Sprinkle over bean dish with nutmeg. Bake 15 minutes or until golden.

When ready to serve, heat rum, ignite and pour over baked beans. Allow flame to burn out before serving.

*FUN COOKING GUIDE: Fix casserole ahead and have ready to bake later. Be a guest at your own party. A company treat, especially for a buffet.

SAUCES

RAISIN SAUCE FOR HAM

1 bottle lemon or lime soda
2 tablespoons apple cider
vinegar
½ cup dark raisins
¼ cup brown sugar

⅛ teaspoon salt
⅛ teaspoon ginger
⅛ teaspoon cinnamon
¼ cup water with
1 tablespoon cornstarch

In a saucepan, mix beverage, vinegar, raisins, sugar, salt, and spices. Cook over low heat. Simmer 10 minutes and add water and cornstarch mixture, stirring constantly, until sauce thickens.

HORSERADISH SAUCE
(Especially for Ham)

---

1 cup mayonnaise	½ teaspoon salt
½ cup horseradish	1 cup whipped cream
2 tablespoons sugar	

Combine all, and fold in whipped cream.

PORK CHEESE

---

2 lbs. boneless pork shoulder	1 bay leaf
4 pigs feet, halved lengthwise	1 teaspoon salt
1 medium onion, chopped	⅓ cup apple cider vinegar
2 whole cloves	2 qts. water
6 peppercorns	

Thoroughly scrub pigs feet. In a large kettle combine meats with all ingredients, bring to boiling, reduce heat, cover, and simmer 2 to 21/2 hours or until meats are tender.

Cool mixture. Remove meat from pigs feet, cube all meats. Discard bay leaf, peppercorn and cloves. Return to heat if necessary to reduce liquid to 4 cups. Season again with salt and red pepper to taste. Pack meats into 9x5x3 inch baking pans or use your favorite pans. Pour in the broth. Chill in refrigerator until firm. Discard fat, if any, on top of loaf.

*FUN COOKING GUIDE: *Dressing for cheese loaf:*

1 small onion, thinly sliced	1 teaspoon salt
¼ cup white wine vinegar	1 teaspoon prepared mustard
¼ teaspoon coarsely cracked pepper	

In a bowl combine all the ingredients; let stand 30 minutes. Unmold loaf onto serving platter, arrange red onion slices around platter, pour vinegar dressing over top. Cut loaf with serrated knife.

*FUN COOKING GUIDE: This pork loaf makes good appetizers, and go well with crackers or French bread. Also cut into little squares, serve on platter with tooth picks.

*FUN COOKING GUIDE: To pretty up the loaf, use chopped pimiento or stuffed olives before pouring liquids.

❖ *Meat and Vegetable* ❖ *Combinations*

STUFFED CABBAGE HEAD
(My Third Award Winner)

25 or 30 cabbage leaves
³/₄ cup uncooked rice
1¹/₂ pint boiling water
2 tablespoons bacon drippings
2 medium onion chopped fine
1 stick celery chopped fine
1 cup ground beef
¹/₂ cup choice of ground pork, or
    sausage, or cooked ham,
    chopped fine

1 egg well beaten
¹/₈ teaspoon nutmeg
¹/₄ teaspoon thyme
A large white cotton cloth,
1 teaspoon salt
¹/₂ teaspoon red pepper
1 clove garlic mashed to grate
    about 28 inches square
American or Velveeta cheese

Immerse cabbage leaves in salted boiling water; cook 2 or 3 minutes or until wilted, adding only a few at a time. Avoid crowding; drain and cool.

Cook rice in boiling salted water 12 minutes; drain and put rice in a large bowl.

Cook ground pork in bacon grease 20 minutes, stirring occasionally. Add salt, pepper, garlic, onion and celery; cook 5 minutes longer. Pour into cooked rice.

Combine rice, pork mixture ham, ground beef, nutmeg, thyme, and egg; mix well and add more salt and pepper if necessary.

Spread out the cloth. In center, place 4 cabbage leaves, to later resemble growing end of a cabbage. Place about 1 tablespoon of mixture in center of each leaf, spread a bit.

Continue building up the head, using up the least attractive leaves first, and placing dressing over each. Then at the last try and cover top and sides with the more perfect leaves, having used up all of the dressing in center.

Bring up all 4 corners of the cloth, and tie a string tightly and closely to the cabbage.

In a large pot, pour 1 pint or more of water; place a rack or lots of crumbled aluminum foil in bottom. Place wrapped cabbage on rack. Cover with a tight-fitting lid; cook over medium heat. When water comes to a boil, reduce heat and cook 1 hour.

When it is done, turn off heat and let set, covered for 10 minutes. Then untie string, unwrap, grate cheese over top, cover again a couple of minutes, then gently lift out cloth and slip onto a platter.

Serve sliced in wedges, cut like a cake; pass your favorite tomato sauce over each helping.

*FUN COOKING GUIDE: Be a guest at your own party. Prepare stuffed cabbage hours ahead; chill until 1½ hours before serving, then cook and serve.

CREOLE CABBAGE ROLLS

(2 Servings)

12 or 14 cabbage leaves, may cut large ones in half along thick ridge	1 small onion, chopped fine
	½ shell of a well beaten egg
	1 clove garlic, finely minced
½ pound ground beef	1 teaspoon salt
3 tablespoons bacon grease or sausage drippings	½ teaspoon red pepper
	¾ cup cooked rice

Cook onion and garlic in bacon grease until tender. In a large bowl, thoroughly mix meat, rice, egg, salt, pepper, and cooked onion. Place about 1 tablespoon of the mixture in soft end of the cabbage, ending with the large end of the leaf. Continue until all are rolled.

In a saucepan that has a tight-fitting lid, place a pan rack, crumble foil or pieces of cabbage on bottom and add water. Place cabbage rolls "HARD" end down.

1 cup canned whole tomatoes and juice	½ teaspoon red pepper
	1 teaspoon sugar.
1 cup water	juice of half a lemon
1 teaspoon salt	

Combine tomatoes, salt, sugar and pepper. Pour over cabbage; squeeze lemon over all. Skin may also be used. Cover with a tight-fitting lid. Cook 15 minutes, then reduce heat to low. Cook 45 minutes longer.

*FUN COOKING GUIDE: For a different taste treat, cook the cabbage rolls without tomatoes. Add 1½ cup water and lemon juice, a few mint leaves and salt. Make your favorite tomato sauce and spread over them when served. Make an extra recipe - they freeze deliciously.

EGGPLANT AND MEAT ROLL IN SAUCE

(2 Servings)

1 medium sized eggplant	½ an egg shell of beaten egg
1 pint salted water	1 medium onion chopped;
Cooking oil or olive oil	divided in two
1 cup or ½ pound ground beef	3 tablespoons cooked rice
salt and pepper	½ a clove garlic, mashed

SAUCE AND TOPPING:

1 tablespoon cooking oil	a pinch nutmeg
onion	1 tablespoon Parmesan cheese
1 cup tomato sauce, canned	grated
Salt and pepper to taste	6 strips of sliced Velveeta or
½ teaspoon sugar	American cheese
a pinch sweet basil	Paprika

Cut both ends of eggplant; stand up and cut 6 slices ¼ inch thick. Then peel, careful not to break slices. Soak slices in salted water 5 minutes; drain. Heat oil in a large skillet, just enough to grease bottom. Over medium heat, cook each slice until soft, turn with a spatula, place them on a dish.

*FUN COOKING GUIDE: Doesn't matter if they split a little; use anyway.

In a bowl, combine meat, egg, half onion, garlic, rice, salt and pepper. Mix well and make into 6 patties, width of eggplant slice. Place meat pattie in center of each slice, fold over each end, press a little. Set aside and make sauce.

SAUCE:

In a saucepan that covers, combine oil, onion, tomato sauce, sugar, sweet basil, nutmeg, and 1 cup water. Boil over medium heat. Then place stuffed eggplant in sauce, cover with a tight-fitting lid; reduce heat and simmer 20 minutes.

Season with salt and pepper. Place a piece of yellow cheese over each. Sprinkle with paprika. Cover and heat through 1 or 2 minutes.

Sprinkle with Parmesan cheese.

FUN COOKING GUIDE: There will probably be some unpeeled eggplant left over. This will keep many days, if put in a plastic bag in refrigerator. Can be used in so many different ways.

*FUN COOKING GUIDE: Can use leftover cooked ham instead of ground beef. Use 1 slice bread, soaked in ¼ cup milk in place of rice.

SMOTHERED BEEF AND CARROTS

(2 Servings)

¾ pound boneless stew meat,
   cut in serving pieces
3 tablespoons corn oil, or
   substitute
carrots peeled and sliced to
   make 1½ cups

1 small onion chopped
¼ cup water
1 teaspoon salt
⅛ teaspoon red pepper
½ teaspoon sugar.

Season meat with salt and pepper. Add meat to cold oil in a saucepan; cover and cook over medium heat, occasionally adding water, and stirring. Cook 45 minutes or until tender; do not overcook. Add carrots, onion, water, and sugar. Cover and cook slowly for 20 minutes; uncover and cook about 5 minutes longer.

*FUN COOKING GUIDE: For a different taste treat pork and yellow or white turnips cooked this way are delicious.

SMOTHERED HAM AND CABBAGE

(2 Servings)

1 cup precooked ham
4 cups finely shredded cabbage
½ cup water
half an apple, peeled and
chopped

1 small onion, minced
¼ teaspoon red pepper
2 tablespoons bacon drippings
salt to taste

In a saucepan that covers add bacon drippings, ham, cabbage, onion, apple, water and red pepper. Cover and cook over medium heat 10 minutes. Reduce heat and cook until cabbage is tender, uncover and cook about 15 minutes longer, then salt to taste. Very good served with blushing rice. (See Page 72)

*FUN COOKING GUIDE: Fresh lean pork is a delicious substitute for ham; cook till tender, first; then adding the remaining ingredients.

STUFFED MIRLITONS
(French for "Vegetable Pears")

(2 Servings)

2 medium sized mirlitons	**¹⁄₂ cup cooked rice**
¹⁄₂ pound or 1 cup ground beef	**2 tablespoons bread or**
¹⁄₂ teaspoon salt	**cracker crumbs**
¹⁄₄ teaspoon cayenne	**butter**
1 small onion, cut fine	

Cut mirlitons in half lengthwise; cover with salted water in a pot with a tight-fitting lid. Reduce heat to simmer; cook until tender, approximately 30 minutes. Do not overcook.

With a teaspoon, discard seed, scoop out pulp, leaving a ¹⁄₄ inch shell. Place shell on a shallow greased baking dish. Preheat oven 350°

Cook meat and onion with seasoning until tender. Should add water and stir occasionally, brown lightly. Add mirliton pulp, cook 10 minutes longer; blend in the rice. Season again to taste.

Fill shells with the mixture, sprinkle top with crumbs, dot with butter. Bake 15 or 20 minutes.

*FUN COOKING GUIDE: If you desire a casserole, or if the mirlitons are too large, peel and dice them. Cook until tender, drain, and combine with meat mixture. Can serve from top of the stove or pour in a baking dish. Sprinkle with crumbs.

*FUN COOKING GUIDE: Instead of ground meat, can use leftover cooked meat, ground; sausage, ham, pork, shrimp or crabmeat. This makes a delicious dish for the main course.

STUFFED PEPPERS

(2 Servings)

2 medium bell peppers	1 tablespoon of a well beaten
1 small bell pepper, cut in	egg
small pieces	1 tablespoon butter
1 cup ground meat	1 teaspoon salt
3 tablespoons cooking oil or	1/4 teaspoon red pepper
bacon drippings	1/4 teaspoon oregano
1 small onion, finely chopped	Bread crumbs
1 clove garlic, mashed	
2 slices very stale bread	
soaked in 1/4 cup milk	

Cut 2 peppers in half from tip to stem, discard seeds, scoop out pulp; use in dressing, cook peppers in boiling water 2 or 3 minutes, drain and set aside.

In a heavy saucepan, place oil, meat, salt. Cook over medium heat, stirring occasionally, about 15 minutes; add onion, garlic, and small pieces of pepper, cook about 15 minutes longer.

Add soaked bread and milk, stir until well blended, remove from heat and add butter and egg.

Fill peppers with the mixture, sprinkle top with bread crumbs. Preheat oven 350°F. Arrange peppers in a shallow baking dish, pour 1/2 cup water around peppers, add about 1 tablespoon cooking fat. Bake 20 or 25 minutes.

*FUN COOKING GUIDE: 1/2 cup cooked rice can be used instead of bread, especially left-over rice, but do not use milk.

STUFFED TOMATOES

(2 Servings)

2 medium tomatoes	2 slices stale bread, soaked
1 cup ground pork	in 1/4 cup milk
2 tablespoons cooking oil	1 tablespoon butter
1 small onion, chopped fine	1/4 teaspoon sugar
1 teaspoon salt	1 tablespoon of a well
1/4 teaspoon red pepper	beaten egg
1/4 teaspoon thyme	1/4 cup bread crumbs

To prepare tomatoes for stuffing, drop them whole in boiling water for 2 minutes; take out and cool in cold water. Peel off skin with a paring knife; cut in half from top to stem; then cut around, leaving all of the outside pulp. This loosens the inside. Then, with a teaspoon, scoop out all of pulp and seeds, which are to be used in the dressing; set aside. Sprinkle sugar with your fingers on inside of the tomatoes to be stuffed.

In a skillet with a heavy bottom, add oil, meat, salt and pepper. Cook over medium heat 5 minutes; reduce heat; cover and cook about 20 minutes longer, adding water occasionally. Smother, but do not fry meat dry. Add onion, stirring almost constantly, cook about 3 minutes. Add pulp from inside of tomatoes, cook 5 minutes longer, or until most of the moisture is cooked out. Add butter and bread soaked in milk, cook and stir until well-blended. Take pot off the stove and add egg mixture.

Fill tomatoes with dressing mixture, sprinkle top with breadcrumbs, arrange on baking dish, pour ½ cup water around tomatoes. Bake in oven preheated to 350° for 30 minutes. Serve as main dish; white beans are a good companion.

*FUN COOKING GUIDE: The tomatoes can be stuffed long before ready for baking; then chilled, to be baked later.

*FUN COOKING GUIDE: Leftover ham is very good to use instead of pork.

STUFFED WHITE SQUASH

(2 Servings)

2 tender medium sized squash
  (white scallops)
¾ cup ground beef
2 tablespoons cooking fat

1 small onion cut fine
2 tablespoons bread crumbs
salt and pepper to taste

Boil squash in plenty of water until tender, not over tender. Cut in half, across scallop. Place on a greased shallow baking sheet, Scoop out pulp being careful not to break the shell, leaving about a ¼ inch shell. (If the squash is young the seeds are edible, otherwise, discard seed.) Set pulp aside.

In a skillet, cook the meat in oil over medium heat about 15 or 20 minutes. Add water and stir occasionally; brown very lightly, add onion, cook until tender. Add squash pulp, cook 2 or 3 minutes or until most of the liquid is cooked out. Season with salt and pepper. Spoon mixture into shells; top with bread crumbs. Preheat oven 350°. Bake 15 minutes.

*FUN COOKING GUIDE: If you prefer, or if the squash are large, squash and meat dish can be made into a casserole. Peel and dice squash; boil in very little water until tender; drain and cook with meat as for stuffing. Pour into a greased casserole; sprinkle with bread crumbs, bake; this may also be served from the skillet.

TOP-OF-STOVE BELL PEPPER
DRESSING

(2 Servings)

2 medium sized bell peppers,
  cut in small pieces
1 cup or ½ pound ground pork
  (can use sausage)
1 small onion, chopped
1 clove garlic, minced
2 slices very stale bread,
  soaked in ¼ cup milk

1 teaspoon salt
¼ teaspoon red pepper
1 tablespoon butter
¼ teaspoon thyme or sage
1 tablespoon of well beaten egg
bread crumbs

Using a heavy skillet, place meat, oil, salt, and pepper; cook over medium heat 5 minutes, stirring occasionally. Reduce heat to low and cook about 20 minutes longer, adding water when needed. Do not fry, but smother, adding water a little at a time.

Add chopped peppers, onion and garlic; cook about 10 minutes or until tender. Stir in the bread soaked in milk, butter and spices; stir; then add egg; cover with a tight-fitting lid. and cook 5 minutes. Top with bread crumbs. Serve hot.

*FUN COOKING GUIDE: This can be baked in a casserole.

*FUN COOKING GUIDE: Can use chopped cooked ham instead of pork, but do not cook as long as pork.

WIENERS AND SAUERKRAUT-MIT-APFEL

(2 Servings)

½ pound wieners cut in
1 inch pieces
2 tablespoons bacon drippings
1 small apple, peeled and
    cut in small pieces
½ teaspoon sugar

1 small onion, cut in
    small pieces
1 small Irish potato grated
1½ cups sauerkraut
½ teaspoon carraway seeds

Cook wieners, apples, potatoes, and onions in the bacon grease 10 to 12 minutes; then add sauerkraut, sugar and carraway seeds. Cover with a tight-fitting lid; reduce heat and cook about 15 minutes longer.

FUN COOKING GUIDE: For a different taste treat use diced cooked ham instead of wieners or both.

❖ *Leftover Dishes* ❖

BEEF AND EGGPLANT CASSEROLE

(2 Servings)

1½ cup diced leftover roast
1½ cup cracker crumbs
1½ cup boiled eggplant
1½ stick butter
1 small onion, chopped

1 tablespoon flour
1 cup water
2 drops hot Tabasco
salt and pepper to taste

Melt butter, add chopped onion and cook until tender and golden brown, stirring constantly. Stir in flour, blending well. Add meat, eggplant, and water. Simmer a few minutes, stirring occasionally. Add salt, pepper and Tabasco.

Into a greased, casserole arrange alternate layers of cracker crumbs, meat and eggplant mixture. Continue until all is used. Bake in 350° oven for 20 minutes.

CHICKEN CROQUETTES

(2 Servings)

1 cup minced cooked chicken
1 cup stale bread crumbs
   moistened in ¼ cup well
   seasoned stock
1 egg beaten, reserve 2 tablespoons mix with 2 tablespoons
   milk to coat croquettes

2 tablespoons butter
2 tablespoons grated onion
½ teaspoon dry mustard
   pinch oregano
salt and pepper to taste

With melted butter in a saucepan, add onion and cook until lightly browned; add bread with stock; stir until bread mixture leaves side of pan.

To the bread mixture add, chicken, egg, mustard and oregano; mix well; salt and pepper to taste.

Divide into 4 equal portions, shape like cones or croquettes; let stand to dry a few minutes.

Pat egg and milk mixture around balls, toss into cracker crumbs and chill in refrigerator until ready to fry. Fry in deep, hot fat until nicely browned.

*FUN COOKING GUIDE: Suggest serving with egg sauce.

CORN BEEF HASH

(2 Servings)

½ a 12 ounce can corn beef,
12 oz size, cut meat in
   small pieces
1 small potato peeled and
   diced in small pieces
2 tablespoons cooking oil
   pinch oregano

2 heaping tablespoons
all-purpose flour
1 small onion, chopped
1 small clove garlic, mashed
1½ cup water
Salt and pepper to taste

Heat oil in a saucepan. Add flour; stir constantly, cooking over low heat until golden brown. Remove saucepan or skillet from heat for fear of burning, add onion, stirring; cook about 5 minutes.

Add meat, potatoes, garlic, and water; place pan over medium heat. When hash comes to a hard boil, reduce heat, cover with a lid and cook 15 minutes; uncover; add oregano; salt and pepper to taste. Cook a bit longer or until potatoes are done.

*FUN COOKING GUIDE: Most leftover cooked meats can be used for hash.

May use other half of corn beef on sandwiches or corn beef and cabbage dish.

HAM CROQUETTES

(2 Servings)

1 cup coarsely ground
   ham
½ cup cracker crumbs,
   or meal
1½ tablespoons butter
2 tablespoons chopped onion
1½ tablespoons all-purpose
   flour

½ cup milk
½ tablespoon prepared mustard
pinch powdered clove
½ shell beaten egg
2 tablespoons beaten egg for
   coating
¼ cup bread crumbs

Cook onion in butter until tender; add flour and blend well; add milk and stir till thick and smooth; set aside to cool. Combine ham, sauce, mustard, egg, clove, cracker crumbs, salt and pepper to taste. Shape into 4 equal sized croquettes.

Coat them with egg, then lightly with bread crumbs; chill in refrigerator a few hours.

Fry in hot fat till golden brown. Drain on paper towel. Serve hot with egg sauce, or they are delicious served plain, or with your favorite sauce.

EGG SAUCE

1½ tablespoons butter
1½ tablespoons all-purpose flour
1 cup milk

1 hard boiled egg, minced
½ teaspoon horseradish

Melt butter; blend in flour and stir; add milk; cook until smooth and thick. Season with salt and pepper; add horseradish and egg. Serve over ham croquettes.

HAM HASH

(2 Servings)

1 cup potatoes, peeled and
   diced
1 cup diced cooked ham
2 tablespoons cooking oil
2 tablespoons all-purpose
   flour

1 small clove garlic, mashed
   (optional)
Salt and pepper to taste
1½ cups water

Make a roux by heating oil in a skillet, add flour, stir constantly over medium heat until golden brown. Remove from heat for fear of burning. Add onion, stirring, cook until soft. Put skillet back over heat, add ham, potatoes and water. When it comes to a hard boil, reduce heat, and cover. Cook 15 to 18 minutes. Season with salt and pepper.

GROUND MEAT HASH

1 cup ground beef
1 cup potatoes, diced
2 cups water
2 tablespoons cooking oil
2 tablespoons all-purpose flour

1 small onion, chopped
If you like the taste of garlic,
   1 clove mashed
Salt and pepper to taste

FUN COOKING GUIDE: Make ground meat hash as the ham hash, but cook 20 minutes.

IRISH POTATO SURPRISE

1½ cup boiled, mashed potatoes	¼ cup leftover peas
salt and pepper to taste	¼ cup flour
2 tablespoons milk	half a shell of 1 beaten egg
1 tablespoon butter	mixed with 2 tablespoons
2 tablespoons minced onion	milk
1 tablespoon minced parsley	¼ cup bread or cracker crumbs

Combine all first 7 ingredients in a mixing bowl; mix well. Divide into 6 equal parts; make an indentation in center of each. Place about a teaspoon of peas, bring potatoes over and make croquettes.

Coat each with flour, then with egg and milk mixture, using your finger tips, then coat with crumbs. Chill several hours, then fry brown in deep fat.

*FUN COOKING GUIDE: Any leftover vegetable or ham is delicious; also leftover beef or pork can be used in this dish instead of peas.

CASSEROLE WITH LEFTOVER VEGETABLES

(2 Servings)

1½ cup any leftover vegetables,	1 cup milk
mixture of any combinations	¼ teaspoon salt
such as broccoli, green beans,	½ teaspoon horseradish
asparagus, carrots, or peas	2 tablespoons bread crumbs
2 tablespoons butter	Yellow cheese, grated
2 tablespoons flour	

Preheat oven 375°. Make a sauce by adding flour to melted butter. Cook over low heat, blend well, add cold milk immediately; stir until smooth and thickened; add salt and horseradish.

Put vegetables in a small baking dish greased with butter; pour sauce over all, sprinkle with crumbs, then with cheese, bake 15 or 20 minutes.

PORK AND NOODLE CASSEROLE

(2 Servings)

1½ cup cooked leftover pork	2 tablespoons bread crumbs
1 cup egg noodles	1 small onion, chopped fine
½ cup cream of mushroom soup	½ cup cheddar cheese
½ cup milk	a few dashes paprika
¼ cup celery, cut fine	a few dashes nutmeg

Cook noodles in 4 cups boiling water 18 to 20 minutes, drain and place in a large mixing bowl. Salt and pepper to taste. Combine pork, noodles, soup, milk, celery, onions, and nutmeg. Mix well and pour in a well buttered deep baking dish. Sprinkle with breadcrumbs and cheese, then with paprika. Bake in 350° preheated oven 30 to 35 minutes or until well browned.

TURKEY STEW

(2 Servings)

1½ cup leftover cooked turkey, cut in small pieces	1 stick celery cut in small pieces
2 tablespoons cooking oil or leftover turkey gravy	¼ cup grated carrots
1 small onion, chopped	½ teaspoon Worcestershire sauce
¾ cup whole tomatoes, canned or fresh	salt and pepper to taste
½ teaspoon sugar	⅓ cup boiled sweetpeas

Cook onion in oil or gravy, until tender. Add tomatoes; cook 5 minutes; add turkey, celery, sugar, 1 cup water; cook 15 minutes.

Add carrots and peas, cook 10 minutes longer; salt and pepper to taste.

*FUN COOKING GUIDE: May make ahead of time and set aside. This will improve the flavor. Reheat.

TURKEY TREAT ON TOAST

(2 Servings)

1½ cups cooked diced turkey
3 tablespoons butter or
   substitute
1 small onion, minced
2 tablespoons chopped celery
2 tablespoons all-purpose flour
1 cup turkey broth
¼ cup evaporated milk
   paprika

salt and pepper to taste
   (depends on broth)
pinch nutmeg
2 drops Tabasco sauce
4 slices bread toasted on
   both sides
4 slices American or Velveeta
   cheese

In a small saucepan add butter, onion and celery. Cook over low heat until tender, add flour and blend well, add turkey broth and milk, cook stirring constantly until sauce thickens, season with salt pepper, nutmeg, and Tabasco sauce; add turkey.

Place the toast on a cookie sheet, pour turkey mixture over each piece then place a slice of cheese over each, sprinkle with a dusting of paprika. Place under the broiler for 2 or 3 minutes or until cheese is bubbly. Do not put turkey mixture on toast until ready to serve.

*FUN COOKING GUIDE: Sauce can be made ahead of serving time.

For a different taste treat, add mushrooms, pimiento, peas, or carrots to the turkey treat.

TURKEY BONE GUMBO

(4 Servings)

½ cup cooking oil
¼ cup all-purpose flour
1 medium onion, chopped
1 clove garlic, minced
3½ pint turkey broth
1½ cup chopped turkey
½ pound smoked sausage or
  ½ pound country pork sausage
  cut in bite size

Salt and red pepper to taste
1 teaspoon each chopped
  parsley and green onion
  tops
Gumbo filé

In a large pot with a heavy bottom, make a roux by heating oil; add flour; cook over low heat, stirring constantly until golden brown (a deep brown); add onion; take pot away from heat, for fear of burning. Stir and cook until onion is tender, about 3 minutes.

Add turkey broth; put pot over medium heat, stirring; when gumbo comes to a rolling boil, add sausage (if you will use same); cover with a tight-fitting lid. Simmer 45 minutes, add turkey, cook 15 minutes longer. Add parsley and onion tops. Serve in soup plates, with cooked rice. If you desire added flavor add ½ teaspoon gumbo filé, in each dish.

*FUN COOKING GUIDE: For a different taste treat instead of sausage use about 6 oysters per servings. Add only a minute or two before serving. Oysters are done when edges curl.

TURKEY SOUFFLÉS WITH GIBLET GRAVY

1½ cup chopped cooked turkey
1¼ cup milk
½ cup turkey broth
⅓ cup yellow cornmeal

¼ teaspoon salt
3 tablespoons butter
2 egg yolks
2 stiffly beaten egg whites

Preheat oven 375°F. Combine cornmeal and broth, mix well. Rinse a small saucepan with cold water, then add milk and butter; heat; add cornmeal and broth mixture; stir constantly and cook until it thickens; set aside to cool.

Combine well beaten egg yolk, turkey and cooked cornmeal, mix well, then fold in the stiffly beaten egg whites. Turn into a well-greased quart-sized baking dish. Set the dish in a larger pan or skillet of warm water.

Bake 35 or 40 minutes, or until top is golden. Serve with giblet gravy.

GIBLET GRAVY

¼ cup chopped cooked giblets
3 tablespoons fat, drippings
　　from turkey
a small piece onion, chopped

1 cup turkey broth or water
1 tablespoon cornstarch,
　　mixed with ¼ cup water

In a small saucepan combine fat, drippings, giblets and onion; cook about 5 minutes; add broth, when it comes to a boil, stir in the cornstarch and water, stir and cook until mixture comes to a boil. Season with salt and pepper. Serve over soufflé.

*FUN COOKING GUIDE; Leftover chicken may be used instead of turkey.

RICE, CABBAGE AND HAM DRESSING

1 cup cooked ham cut in bits
4 cups chopped cabbage
1 cup cooked rice
2 tablespoons cooking oil

2 tablespoons chopped apple
1 medium onion, chopped
Salt and pepper to taste

Cook ham in oil about 10 minutes, stirring occasionally. Add half the onion and apple, cook 5 minutes over low heat. Take out cooked ham mixture on a warm platter, leaving drippings in pot. To the drippings add cabbage, remaining onion, and ¼ cup water. Cover with a tight-fitting lid and cook 20 minutes longer.

Stir in the rice and ham mixture. Heat thoroughly, about 5 minutes. Serve hot or at room temperature.

*FUN COOKING GUIDE: For this dish, leftover pork is fine as a substitute for the ham.

Use as a main dish.

RICE, BLACKEYED PEAS AND HAM DRESSING

½ cup cooked ham, cut in bits
½ cup cooked leftover
　　blackeye peas
1 cup cooked rice

2 tablespoons cooking oil
1 medium onion, chopped
Salt and pepper to taste

*FUN COOKING GUIDE: Cook as for cabbage and ham recipe. Use as a main dish.

❖ Vegetables ❖

BLACKEYED PEAS

1 cup dried blackeyed peas
4 cups water
½ teaspoon sugar

1 small onion, chopped
1 small piece salt meat, or ham

Wash peas; combine in a saucepan with water, half of the onions, sugar, and salt meat; cover with a tight-fitting lid and simmer over low fire 1 hour. Add remaining onion and cook 20 minutes longer.

*FUN COOKING GUIDE: Never boil peas or beans over a high fire as this tears them up and they are not tasty.

*FUN COOKING GUIDE: Eat dried peas and beans with comfort. If you will follow these directions, you will not have any discomfort. In a large pot of boiling water, add washed and drained peas or beans. Let them come to a hard boil for about two or three minutes. Let them soak in this water for eight hours or overnight Then drain and rinse and drain again. Add them to boiling water again. Always simmer: do not boil them. Season according to recipe.

*FUN COOKING GUIDE: Of course some of the nutritious vitamins may be lost, but at least there are plenty of protein in them.

RED BEANS AND RICE

1 pound dried red beans or
  kidney beans
1 large hamhock from leftover
  ham, or sausage
2 tablespoons margarine
  or ham fat
1 large onion finely chopped
  whole tomatoes

Pick and wash red beans.
1 or 2 clove garlic finely minced
1 teaspoon salt
¼ teaspoon red pepper
1 small piece bay leaf
½ teaspoon oregano powder
  2 large ripe tomatoes or canned

In a large saucepan broil 1½ quarts water, drop in the beans, boil 1 minute. Set aside until they cool. Cook onion in fat until tender. Add to beans, with garlic, hamhock, tomatoes, bayleaf, salt and pepper. Cook over high heat, then reduce to simmer until tender, about 2½ to 3 hours.

Take out hamhock, cut meat away from bone. Add to pot of beans and add oregano. Discard bone. Serve in soup plates with a serving of rice. (Page 72-73) Chopped scallions over this is delicious.

*FUN COOKING GUIDE: If using sausage, do not cook them longer than 1 hour. If there are leftover beans, chill in individual servings and freeze.

GREAT NORTHERN BEANS

1 cup dried "Great Northern beans"	1 onion, medium chopped divide into 2 portions
¼ pound salt meat or a ham bone	½ teaspoon brown sugar 5 cups water

Wash beans thoroughly. Put beans, water, pork, sugar and half onion in a saucepan and bring to boil. Reduce heat and cover with a tight-fitting lid and allow to simmer very slowly for 1 1/2 hours, or until tender. Add remaining onion., salt and pepper and continue to simmer for 15 minutes.

CAUTION: Never boil over high heat, as beans may break or burn.

*FUN COOKING GUIDE: These beans may be cooked hours before meal, as this will improve flavor.

CREOLE GREEN BEANS
(Makes 2 Servings)

½ pound fresh snap beans	1 cup boiling water
4 or 5 new potatoes, soaked in water with a little soda, then scraped	3 tablespoons bacon drippings 1 teaspoon sugar
1 small onion, chopped	½ teaspoon salt ¼ teaspoon black pepper

Combine all the ingredients in a small stew pan; cover with a tight-fitting lid; cook over medium heat 5 minutes. Reduce heat; cook about 15 minutes longer. The beans should be tender crisp.

GREEN BEANS WITH HORSERADISH SAUCE

Prepare green beans as snap beans above; but omit bacon drippings. After cooking, drain off liquid.

SAUCE:

1½ tablespoons butter or margarine   1 tablespoon grated onion
1½ tablespoons all-purpose flour   ¼ teaspoon prepared mustard
¾ cup milk   ½ teaspoon prepared horseradish

Sauté onion in butter, add flour, stir, then add milk. Cook until smooth and thick; add horseradish and mustard. Pour sauce over heated beans. Serve hot

CREAMED BROCCOLI
(New Version of Cream Sauce)

(Makes 4 Servings)

1 package fresh frozen broccoli   ¾ cup milk, sweet
1 heaping tablespoon butter   Salt and pepper to taste
1 tablespoon minced onion   American or Velveeta cheese,
1 tablespoon chopped celery   grated
½ slice bread   Dusting of paprika

Boil broccoli according to directions on package, drain and set aside. Soak bread in milk, about 5 minutes; set aside. Cook onion and celery in butter until tender, stirring constantly; add bread and milk, cooking over low heat until it comes to a boil. Salt and pepper to taste.

Preheat oven 350°.

Place cooked broccoli in a small baking dish; pour sauce over all; grate cheese over sauce; dust with paprika. Bake about 15 minutes, or until cheese is bubbly.

*FUN COOKING GUIDE: Many vegetables can be used instead of broccoli, such as cauliflower, asparagus or cabbage.

*FUN COOKING GUIDE: So many of my retired senior citizen friends who live alone, or working people say, "Oh, I don't cook because it's always too much for me." Well, I prepare any cooked recipe that is in this book, chill it, then place individual servings in a sandwich bag. Freeze on a tray, then put servings in a bread or plastic bag. Label inside so you can read it as such:

When needed, either frozen or defrosted contents may be put in a wide-mouth jar and heated on top of the stove or in a pan of water. Grease the jar before adding the contents. SAVES ENERGY AND TIME.

*FUN COOKING GUIDE: **Fresh Fruit All Year Round** - Add peaches to boiling water then put them in ice water. Skin them, do not peel, then slice or wedge. Put on a waxed paper covered cookie sheet and freeze. When frozen put in plastic bag or container for the freezer. All berries can be frozen first on a waxed paper covered cookie sheet before bagging them and this will keep them whole, not mashed.

PURPLE CABBAGE WITH APPLES

(2 Servings)

2 cups finely shredded purple cabbage,
1 small apple, unpeeled, cut in small pieces
2 tablespoons bacon grease

1 small onion, chopped fine
¼ teaspoon prepared mustard
½ teaspoon sugar
1 teaspoon tarragon vinegar

Place bacon grease, onion, and apple in a saucepan; cook 4 or 5 minutes, stirring occasionally. Add cabbage, cover tightly, and cook over very low heat 20 minutes. Add sugar, mustard and vinegar; cook 2 or 3 minutes longer. Serve while hot.

*FUN COOKING GUIDE: For both economy and preserved flavor, store vegetable in refrigerator immediately after purchasing. Also, to get most nutrition from cabbage, always cook in boiling water, never in cold at the start. Eat them for pleasure and not for duty.

BOILED CABBAGE

Cut very thin wedges of cabbage. Place in plenty of salted boiling water for 20 minutes. Drain off liquid. Add 2 tablespoons butter, salt and black pepper and a little vinegar.

CABBAGE WITH CREAM SAUCE

(4 Servings)

3 cups shredded cabbage

Cook in salted boiling water 7 minutes, drain and pour into a small shallow baking dish, greased.

SAUCE:

1½ tablespoons butter	**salt and pepper to taste**
1½ tablespoon all-purpose flour	**grated yellow cheese for topping**
¾ cup milk	**paprika**

In a saucepan, add flour to melted butter, blend well. Add milk, stir constantly, and cook until smooth. Salt and pepper to taste. Pour sauce over cabbage, a little cheese over top; dust with paprika. Bake in oven preheated to 350° for 15 minutes.

*FUN COOKING GUIDE: This cabbage dish can be made and served from the top of the stove. Cook cabbage and add to sauce, sprinkle with cheese.

CURRIED CABBAGE

Cook cabbage as above. Make white sauce; add to it ¼ teaspoon curry powder, combine with cabbage and serve hot.

BOILED CABBAGE WITH SALT MEAT

Cook a piece of salt meat, weighing ½ pound, in water to cover, about 1 hour, or until tender. Add wedges of cabbage. Cook 15 minutes. Serve. For a taste treat, squeeze juice of half a lemon, or a tablespoon of apple cider vinegar.

CORN BEEF AND CABBAGE

(2 Servings)

½ a 12 ounce can corn beef	**1 quart boiling salted water**
4 wedges cabbage	**a couple dashes ginger powder**

Cook cabbage in boiling water for 15 minutes; drain off liquid. Place cabbage in a greased baking dish that covers; sprinkle with ginger, place corn beef over cabbage, cover and bake 10 or 15 minutes. If you prefer, serve with apple cider, vinegar, or lemon.

Boiled potatoes are a good companion to this dish.

*FUN COOKING GUIDE: Before cutting cabbage wedges, cut out a few leaves to make stuffed cabbage head or rolls very soon. Also, keep part of the center for salad or cole slaw.

*FUN COOKING GUIDE: The canned corn beef is very rich. May use other half of can to make corn beef hash or, cut for sandwiches.

CARROT FRITTERS

(2 Servings)

2 or 3 carrots boiled in plenty of water. Peel and mash to make 1 cup	$\frac{1}{4}$ teaspoon salt
	1 teaspoon sugar
	1 teaspoon vanilla
2 tablespoons all-purpose flour	cooking oil to cover small
$\frac{1}{2}$ teaspoon baking powder	skillet $\frac{1}{2}$ inch
1 tablespoon of well beaten egg	

Combine all the ingredients in a bowl, beat until smooth.

Heat oil; drop batter by tablespoons; fry to a golden brown, turning once. Drain on absorbent paper. Serve at once.

CARROT AND PINEAPPLE FRITTERS

(2 Servings)

1 cup cooked mashed carrots	1 tablespoon of a well beaten egg
3 tablespoons crushed pineapple, drained well	$\frac{1}{4}$ teaspoon salt
3 tablespoons all-purpose flour	cooking oil to cover small
$\frac{1}{2}$ teaspoon baking powder	skillet $\frac{1}{2}$ inch

Combine all the ingredients in a bowl; beat until smooth. Heat oil in a small skillet; drop mixture by tablespoonful; fry to a golden brown, turning once. Drain on absorbent paper towel. Serve at once.

*FUN COOKING GUIDE: Batter can be made hours before serving time; chill. Flavor and texture will improve.

BAKED CHEESE CARROTS

(2 Servings)

Scrape or peel 3 or 4 carrots, cook in plenty of water until tender crisp. Drain. Slice carrots in long ¼ inch thick strips; arrange them in a shallow buttered baking dish; sprinkle a little sugar, top with grated American or Velveeta cheese. Add 2 tablespoons melted butter.

*FUN COOKING GUIDE: Do not use salt Preheat oven 400°. Bake about 15 minutes, serve at once.

CARROT CRISP

(2 Servings)

1½ cup thinly sliced carrots	¼ cup powdered milk
½ cup water	1 teaspoon sugar
2 tablespoons butter	salt and pepper

Combine carrots, water, and sugar in saucepan; cook over medium heat 5 minutes; reduce heat to low; cook 15 minutes longer or until tender crisp; add butter, milk, salt and pepper, heat thoroughly and serve.

BAKED CARROT RING

(4 Servings)

2 cups grated carrots	3 eggs, beaten
1 small onion, chopped	3 tablespoons melted butter
2 cups milk	or substitute
½ cup cracker crumbs	

Cook carrots in a little boiling water 3 minutes. Drain, mix carrots with remaining ingredients. Pour in well greased ring mold. Place in a pan of hot water and bake in a preheated oven at 350° for 45 minutes. To unmold run knife around mold and invert on a platter and fill center with buttered green peas.

BLUSHING CAULIFLOWER

(2 Servings)

1½ cups cauliflowerettes
2 tablespoons olive oil or
   melted butter
Salt and pepper

3 tablespoons apple cider vinegar
Paprika

Cook cauliflower in plenty of boiling salted water 15 minutes or until just done; drain; spoon oil or butter over all. Salt and pepper to taste. Pour vinegar over them. Sprinkle with paprika; they will blush. Serve at room temperature as a salad.

*FUN COOKING GUIDE: Always add the vegetables to boiling water for tender crispness.

CAULIFLOWER AND CARROTS

(2 Servings)

1 cup cauliflowerettes
½ cup sliced carrots
1 teaspoon vinegar

2 tablespoons butter
½ teaspoon sugar
salt and pepper to taste

Break cauliflowerettes to make 1 cup and cook in generous amount of salted boiling water with vinegar for 8 to 10 minutes. Drain off liquid. Cook carrots in ½ cup boiling water in covered pan for 15 minutes. Combine both vegetables, add salt, pepper, butter and sugar; heat thoroughly and serve.

CAULIFLOWER-AU-GRATIN

Break off cauliflower to make
2 cups cauliflowerettes
¾ cup cream of mushroom soup,
  canned
¼ cup milk
1 tablespoon butter
a pinch of nutmeg

2 tablespoons bread or cracker
  crumbs
¼ cup grated American cheese
1 tablespoon butter
¼ teaspoon white pepper
2 dashes Tabasco sauce

Add cauliflower to boiling water. Cook rapidly until tender and crisp; may be done in 15 minutes.

Drain and place in a greased baking dish, sprinkle with a little salt. Combine mushroom soup, milk, Tabasco sauce, pepper and butter.

Heat thoroughly, pour mixture over cauliflower, sprinkle with crumbs, dot with butter, then with cheese. Bake 20 minutes.

*FUN COOKING GUIDE: The cauliflower you do not use in this dish will keep uncooked in refrigerator almost a week if wrapped well.

CELERY LEAF SOUFFLÉ

(6 Servings)

1½ cups celery leaves, cut fine
2 tablespoons butter
1 small onion, chopped fine
2 tablespoons flour
1 cup milk
½ cup cream or evaporated milk

½ teaspoon salt
¼ teaspoon pepper
¼ teaspoon paprika
2 egg yolks
2 stiffly beaten egg whites

Preheat oven to 325°.

To prepare celery leaves, wash and separate. Pile them high on a cutting board, and, holding tight, cut across fine; put in large bowl.

In a saucepan, over medium heat, sauté onion in butter, blend in flour, add milk, stirring constantly until smooth and thickened.

Season with salt and pepper and paprika. Cool slightly.

Add beaten egg yolk to sauce; blend; add celery leaves. Gently fold in stiffly beaten egg whites. Pour into a 1-pint greased baking dish. Place in a pan of warm water. Bake 45 minutes, or until it is done (When a knife comes out clean).

*FUN COOKING GUIDE: This is a delicious vegetable served with fish or meat. Makes a nice company treat.

CELERY VINAIGRETTE

(2 Servings)

¼ cup olive oil	1 teaspoon minced sweet
2 tablespoons apple cider	pickle
vinegar	salt
1 tablespoon minced onion	pepper
1 tablespoon minced parsley	paprika
¼ teaspoon sugar	1 hard-cooked egg, minced
a small piece of pimiento,	
chopped	

Combine all the ingredients; chill before pouring over celery. To prepare celery:

Cut 2 large sticks of celery in 2 inch lengths: Peel out strings of celery. Cook 15 minutes in small amount of chicken broth; drain, and serve with sauce poured over it. Keep at room temperature or chill.

*FUN COOKING GUIDE: Use either canned chicken broth, or boil bony parts of chicken to be used later, for a dish calling for boiled chicken.

MAQUECHOU

4 ears of fresh corn	½ teaspoon salt
2 tablespoons cooking oil	a few dashes white pepper
½ cup milk	a lump butter
1 teaspoon sugar	

Cut, corn from the cob. Scrape cob lengthwise.

In a saucepan add oil, corn, milk and sugar; cook over low heat, stirring almost constantly 20 minutes; then add salt, pepper and butter; cook a minute longer. Serve hot.

*FUN COOKING GUIDE: This corn dish is a very old Indian-Acadian dish. There are several versions of maquechou. Some of the Acadians cooked corn with chicken, and called this poulet maquechou; instead of using milk, some are made with one fresh tomato chopped. So, for a different taste treat make with tomatoes and omit milk.

Chicken maquechou; brown then smother a fryer; add onion; cook until tender.

Dish out, add corn. Cook 20 minutes. Add cooked chicken to corn, stir well.

CORN ON THE COB

(2 Servings)

Remove husk from fresh ears of corn and brush off silk.

Place 2 or more ears in a large kettle, with 1½ cup water and 2 tablespoons sugar. Cover with a tight-fitting lid. Place over a high fire; listen when water comes to a hard boil, reduce heat to simmer; cook for 10 minutes longer, just until milk is set. Do not uncover; turn off heat and let it stay covered 10 minutes longer; salt, pepper and spread soft butter over all.

EGGPLANT AND RICE DRESSING

(4 Servings)

1 small eggplant or 2 cups
   when chopped
1½ cup cooked rice
1 small onion, chopped

1 small piece green pepper
2 tablespoons bacon fat or
   ham drippings

Cut eggplant into small pieces, using the peel also. It is edible and has a lot of food value. Place all the above ingredients, except rice, in a saucepan. Add ½ cup water. Cover and cook over low heat about 20 minutes. Uncover. There should be very little liquid left. Season with salt and pepper. Add rice. Cook 10 minutes. Stir well but do not mash.

*FUN COOKING GUIDE: You may not be able to find a small enough eggplant, so buy next to the smallest and refrigerate uncooked part you won't need today, and use some other day. Try frying eggplant in batter.

For a different treat cook rice and eggplant dressing as above, but pour in a small buttered bake dish, grate yellow cheese over all and bake 5 or 10 minutes.

FRIED EGGPLANT

(2 Servings)

1 small eggplant, or part of a
   medium eggplant
¼ cup flour
½ shell of well beaten egg

2 tablespoons milk
¼ cup cracker meal or crumbs
a few dashes of salt and pepper

Peel eggplant (optional), cut in 1 inch slices. Soak slices in salt water to cover for 15 minutes. Drain well.

Mix egg and, milk. Coat slices with flour, dip in egg and milk mixture; then coat with cracker crumbs. Let rest at room temperature a few minutes.

Fry in hot fat a few at a time to a golden brown on both sides. Serve hot.

*FUN COOKING GUIDE: The slices, when coated with the mixture, can be chilled in refrigerator hours before frying. Be a guest at your own party.

EGGPLANT ITALIENNE

(2 Servings)

1 small eggplant: Washed and cut in small pieces, (peeling is edible)	2 small onion, chopped fine 3 stuffed olives, chopped fine 2 tablespoons Parmesan cheese

Place eggplant in ¼ cup water in a stew pan; cover and cook over low fire 10 minutes. Cook onions in olive oil about 5 minutes. Add to eggplant along with olives, cheese, salt and pepper. Cook 20 minutes over low heat.

*FUN COOKING GUIDE: This recipe makes a delicious dip. If desired, 2 tablespoons tomato sauce may be added.

MUSTARD GREENS, SOUTHERN STYLE

(4 Servings)

1 bundle fresh mustard greens, washed well and drained ¼ pound salt pork 1 tablespoon shortening	1 tablespoon flour 1 small onion, chopped fine salt and pepper to taste

Boil pork in 1 pint of water until tender, cover with a lid while cooking and reduce heat to simmer. Add greens and cook until tender, about 20 minutes. Chop greens and pork, drain off liquid and reserve 1 cup.

In a saucepan, add flour to heated oil, cook, stirring constantly, until light brown; remove from heat; add onion; cook until tender. Add pork, greens and liquid. When it comes to a hard boil, cover and reduce heat to simmer; cook 20 minutes. Good served with corn bread or spoon bread.

*FUN COOKING GUIDE: Almost any green can be used for this dish.

SPINACH FOR A TREAT

(4 Servings)

1 pound fresh spinach, washed well and drained	1 small onion, grated
2 slices bacon	1 clove garlic
2 tablespoons butter	¾ cup milk
1½ tablespoons all-purpose flour	1 hard boiled egg, minced

Boil 2 cups water with ½ teaspoon salt; add spinach, cover and cook 20 minutes. Drain off liquid; chop spinach, and set aside.

Fry bacon crisp; drain on paper. Crumble and set aside.

In a saucepan, add onion and garlic to butter, cook, stirring constantly until tender; add flour, blend well; add milk, cook stirring until thickened. Add chopped spinach, cook 2 or 3 minutes.

Serve topped with bacon and egg.

*FUN COOKING GUIDE: This dish is eaten for pleasure and not for duty. Can also use canned or frozen spinach.

FRIED GRITS

(2 Servings)

1½ cup grits, white or yellow	1 teaspoon butter or margarine
2 cups water	¼ cup flour
½ teaspoon salt	½ shell of beaten egg
	paprika

Boil water with salt, then gradually add grits stirring constantly. Reduce heat to very low, cook slowly 20 or 25 minutes, stirring frequently.

Pour cooked grits into a small greased square dish or jelly glass. Chill in refrigerator.

When cold, cut into 1/2 inch slices; coat all sides slightly with flour, then with finger tips, coat with well beaten egg, can chill again or let rest a few minutes, dust all sides with paprika.

Heat cooking oil in a skillet 1/2 inch deep. Fry a golden brown, turn once and fry.

*FUN COOKING GUIDE: Fried grits is a good accompaniment to liver or almost any meat.

TEXAS FRIED OKRA

(2 Servings)

¾ pound tender okra
3 tablespoons cooking oil
1 small onion chopped
a piece of ripe tomato, chopped

a small piece bell pepper, chopped
¼ cup corn meal
salt and pepper

Cut off both ends of okra and discard; slice the okra across in very thin slices.

In a bowl, combine okra, bell pepper, onion, tomato. Mix well, sprinkle cornmeal over all. Put oil in a heavy skillet with a heavy bottom; heat a bit over medium heat; add okra mixture. Cover and reduce heat to low. Cook about 10 minutes. Uncover, but do not stir, let fry a little while. Then stir, being careful not to break or squash the okra. Altogether, cook 20 or 25 minutes. Serve hot.

*FUN COOKING GUIDE: When purchasing okra, buy a little more, picking extra small pods, either to be used in creole or for salad. Delicious.

SMOTHERED OKRA

(2 Servings)

1 pound tender fresh okra
1 small ripe tomato cut in
   small pieces
1 small onion, chopped fine

1 piece green pepper, chopped
   fine
2 tablespoons cooking oil or
   bacon grease

Wash okra; drain; cut them across in very small slices. In a stew pan that covers, add oil, heat a bit. Add all the ingredients, cover and cook over low heat 10 minutes. Uncover and cook until tender, with not too much moisture, stirring okra occasionally, but do not mash, for it will become slimy. Season with salt and pepper to taste.

*FUN COOKING GUIDE: If there is a small amount of cooked okra leftover, use for chicken, sausage, seafood or shrimp okra gumbo; also allow more to smother for any of these uses. For a different taste treat add diced cooked ham while cooking okra.

CREOLE OKRA

(4 Servings)

½ pound or 2 cups okra. (Use large ones. cut in 1" pieces, or use very small ones whole); cook in plenty salted boiling water 15 minutes, or until just tender; drain off liquid
2 tablespoons butter or meat drippings
1 cup whole tomatoes
2 tablespoons tomato paste with 1 cup water
1 small onion, chopped fine
1 tablespoon celery leaves, chopped fine
a small piece green pepper, chopped fine
1 clove garlic, mashed
¼ teaspoon carraway seeds

Cook onion in butter 2 minutes. Add all the ingredients except okra and carraway seeds. Simmer over low heat 20 minutes. Add okra and seeds; cook 5 minutes longer.

*FUN COOKING GUIDE: For both economy and preserved flavor, store vegetable in refrigerator immediately after purchasing.

FRENCH FRIED ONION RINGS

Slice a large white onion (Do not peel now) ¼ inch thick. Then push out and make into individual rings. Then peel.

¼ cup flour
2 tablespoons evaporated milk
1 tablespoon water
1 egg white partially beaten
¼ cup cracker crumbs
Salt and pepper to taste

Soak onion rings in milk, drain. Salt and pepper the onion rings. Coat well with flour, dip with mixture of water and egg white, then with cracker crumbs. Let set a few minutes.

Fry in deep fat a few minutes to a golden brown. Serve hot.

*FUN COOKING GUIDE: The onion rings can be prepared ahead of serving time and kept in refrigerator until time to serve.

HASH BROWNED POTATOES

(4 Servings)

Potatoes peeled, and sliced to
   make 3 cups (small red
are tastier)
1 medium onion, sliced

¼ cup bacon grease
½ teaspoon salt
black pepper
1 teaspoon all-purpose flour

Combine all ingredients in a bowl; let set 10 minutes. Heat ¼ cup bacon grease or cooking oil in a heavy skillet that has a cover. Pour potato mixture in fat, cover and reduce heat. Cook about 15 minutes or until tender; uncover, cook 2 or 3 minutes longer. Turn potatoes with egg turner or spatula, cook 5 minutes. Sprinkle with paprika, pour off excess grease and serve.

*FUN COOKING GUIDE: For a different taste treat at breakfast, brunch or supper; add one or two well beaten eggs to the potatoes when done; pour over all; cover a minute until eggs are set. Careful not to mash.

BAKED POTATO BOATS

(4 Servings)

4 white Idaho potatoes
4 tablespoons soft butter
¼ cup evaporated milk
1 egg yolk
1 egg white, beaten stiff

salt and pepper to taste
Yellow cheese to grate
   over potatoes
few dashes paprika
4 pieces aluminum foil

Preheat oven to 400°F.

Wash potatoes and wrap each snugly in foil; bake 1 hour.

When not too hot to handle, but still warm, cut potatoes in half, lengthwise; and with a teaspoon, scoop out the pulp, being careful not to break the skin. Mash pulp till creamy, adding buttermilk, salt and pepper; mix well; then add egg yolk. The egg white should be very stiff; then fold into potato mixture.

Pile high and lightly into potato shells; grate a coating of cheese over all; sprinkle with paprika. Bake about 15 minutes.

*FUN COOKING GUIDE: If potato boats are to be served when time will be short, chill or freeze them; then just reheat. For a pretty dish, wrap a foil around shell. Be a guest at your own party!

TOP-OF-STOVE POTATO-AU-GRATIN

(4 Servings)

2 or 3 potatoes to make 2 cups
   when pared and sliced
1 medium onion, chopped fine
½ teaspoon salt
2 tablespoons water
2 tablespoons butter or
   substitute
few dashes black pepper
2 drops Tabasco sauce

2 slices bacon, cut in small
   pieces; pan broil until
   crisp; drain, crumble
¼ cup bread crumbs, fried in
2 tablespoons butter
¼ cup grated sharp cheese
   (yellow)
¼ cup evaporated milk

Combine melted butter, potatoes, onion, salt and water in a heavy skillet; cover with a tight-fitting lid,

Cook over medium heat 10 minutes, or until potatoes are just tender. Add bacon grease.

Add milk and cheese to cooked mixture, toss lightly; cook uncovered 10 minutes.

Meanwhile, heat bread crumbs and butter in another skillet. Toss until lightly browned.

Remove potatoes to a warm platter, and top with crumbs, then bacon. Serve hot.

FRENCH POTATO PUFFS

(2 Servings)

1 cup boiled, mashed potatoes
3 tablespoons butter
2 tablespoons minced onion
⅓ cup all-purpose flour

⅓ cup water
½ teaspoon sugar
¾ teaspoon salt
1 egg, beaten

In a small saucepan, cook onion in butter until tender; stir in the flour; add water, sugar, salt and egg, cook over low heat. Stir fast until thick and glossy. Remove from heat; stir in the potatoes. Set aside to cool.

Shape into small balls; let set at room temperature about 30 minutes. Fry in hot cooking fat, a few at a time, until golden brown. Drain on paper toweling; sprinkle with black pepper. Serve hot.

PARMESAN BROWNED POTATOES

(2 Servings)

2 cups potatoes, peeled and
  sliced thin
3 tablespoons bacon fat, or
  cooking oil

¼ cup grated Parmesan cheese
salt
paprika
garlic powder

Heat bacon fat in a heavy-bottomed saucepan and add potatoes. Cover and cook over medium heat 15 minutes. Uncover and add half the cheese; dust with garlic powder, salt and paprika. Turn over the mixture gently. Add remaining cheese and cook about 8 minutes longer.

*FUN COOKING GUIDE: For a different taste treat, omit cheese and add onion. When done, add a beaten egg. Cook until firm.

GLAZED PUMPKIN

3 heaping cupfuls of pumpkin
  peeled and cut into ½ inch
  squares (do not wash)
½ cup plus 2 tablespoons sugar
2 tablespoons water

½ teaspoon grated orange or
  lemon peel.
A pinch of salt.
¼ teaspoon nutmeg (optional)
1 teaspoon butter

In a saucepan combine pumpkin, water, sugar, salt and grated orange peel over high heat, stirring until sugar melts and syrup comes to a hard boil. Cover with a tight-fitting lid, reduce heat, and cook 10 minutes. Uncover, raise heat, cook 8 to ten minutes longer. Be careful not to stir, but baste with syrup, add butter and nutmeg.

*FUN COOKING GUIDE: Buy as small a pumpkin as possible and wrap remaining part in plastic bag, refrigerate and use later stewed or in pie. For a different taste treat, add your choice - raisins, grapes, coconut, walnuts or pecans just before pumpkin is done.

In a saucepan that covers, combine water, pumpkin, orange or lemon, salt, and sugar, over high heat bring to a rolling boil, reduce heat, cover with a lid and cook 10 minutes. Uncover and cook about 10 minutes longer or until pumpkin is tender, add butter.

Serve as companion to meats.

*FUN COOKING GUIDE: Buy as small a pumpkin as possible and wrap the remaining part in a plastic bag; refrigerate and use later stewed or in pies.

For a different taste treat, add raisins, coconut, walnuts or pecans, nutmeg to the glazed pumpkin just before it is done.

STEWED PUMPKIN

(2 Servings)

**cut and peel part of a pumpkin
to make 2 cups when diced
into small bits**
¼ cup water
a pinch salt

**2 tablespoon sugar, brown or
white**
⅛ teaspoon nutmeg
1 tablespoon butter

Combine pumpkin and water in a stew pan, cover and cook over low heat 10 minutes, or until tender, uncover, add salt, sugar butter and nutmeg, cook 5 or 10 minutes longer, while it cooks stir and mash pulp. Serve with meats.

FUN COOKING GUIDE: If pumpkin is needed for pie; stew as above but omit sugar, nutmeg, and butter. Add what is needed for pie.

BLUSHING RICE

(4 Servings)

1 cup white rice
2 cups water
1 teaspoon salt

1 tablespoon butter
a few dashes paprika

Place water, rice and salt in a heavy 1 quart saucepan, over high heat, bring to a rolling boil, stir, turn heat very low, cover pot with a tight-fitting lid, cook 13 or 14 minutes, remove saucepan from heat (do not uncover or peek) let stand 10 minutes longer. Now the rice is cooked; pour in a serving dish, add butter, stir with a fork, sprinkle with paprika, toss lightly for blushing rice.

Serve with fish or meats.

BOILED RICE

(4 servings)

6 cups water
1 cup white rice

2 teaspoon salt

Bring water with salt to a vigorous boil over high heat, add rice, when water comes to a second boil, reduce heat to simmer, stir with a fork, cook 18 or 20 minutes. Add cold water to fill pot, drain in a collander. After rice is well drained pour in a well buttered pot, and keep warm.

STUFFED YELLOW SQUASH
WITH BACON

3 medium yellow squash
3 slices bacon, fried till crisp,
   drain on paper, reserve fat.
1 small onion, chopped

salt and pepper to taste
Ritz cracker or regular
   cracker crumbs

Boil squash in plenty of salted water about 15 minutes or until just tender; do not overcook. Take them out of water, being careful not to break the neck of the squash. Cut them in half lengthwise, on through the neck. With a teaspoon, scoop out pulp (seeds, if tender are edible) for the filling; set aside. Place squash shells on a shallow greased, baking dish.

In a small saucepan, cook onion with bacon drippings until tender. Add squash pulp, cook until most of the moisture is cooked out. Spoon mixture into the 6 shells, sprinkle Ritz crumbs over all, then the crumbled bacon.

Preheat oven 350°. Bake about 10 minutes.

*FUN COOKING GUIDE: This dish can be made and served from the top of the stove. Dice squash and boil in very little water in a covered stew pan until tender; drain and set aside; add to cooked onion. Smother the boiled squash, then add the fried bacon; serve. Or make into a casserole by pouring into a small greased baking dish; top with crumbs and bake 10 or 15 minutes.

STUFFED YELLOW SQUASH (LONG NECK) WITH CORN

3 medium squash
2 tablespoons butter
1 small onion, chopped fine
half clove garlic, minced
½ cup canned whole kernel
  corn; drain off liquid

¼ cup cracker crumbs
grated yellow cheese
  (American, or Velveeta)
dusting of paprika

Boil squash in plenty of salted water for 15 minutes or until just tender; do not overcook, take squash out of water, being careful not to break neck. Cool. Cut squash in half lengthwise through the neck. Scoop out pulp, leaving ¼ inch shell. Place on a greased baking sheet. Reserve pulp; seeds are also edible.

In a small saucepan, sauté onion and garlic in butter until tender, stirring constantly. Add squash, cook until most of the moisture is out, then add corn. Pour mixture into shells, top with cracker crumbs, then grate cheese over all. Bake in 350° oven 10 or 15 minutes.

*FUN COOKING GUIDE: Squash and corn can be made into a casserole: dice the squash in small bits, the size of peas, boil in a little water, drain and fix as above.

Can be fixed ahead of time and chilled before baking.

BAKED TOMATO CUSTARD

(2 Servings)

1½ cups whole tomatoes
  chopped (canned or fresh,
  overripe)
1 egg, beaten slightly
2 tablespoons melted butter
1 small onion, grated

½ teaspoon sugar
½ teaspoon celery seed
salt and pepper to taste
½ cup cracker crumbs
yellow cheeese to grate
dusting of paprika

Preheat oven 350°.

In a large mixing bowl, combine all ingredients except cheese and paprika. Mix well and pour in a deep baking dish, greased. Grate cheese over all; dust with paprika. Bake 30 minutes.

*FUN COOKING GUIDE: This is a good vegetable companion to serve with fish.

GRILLED TOMATOES

(2 Servings)

1 or 2 ripe tomatoes, cut in
   ½ inch slices
salt and pepper to taste
½ teaspoon sugar

approximately ¼ cup fine
   cracker crumbs
melted butter
dusting of paprika

Season tomato slices with salt, pepper and sugar. Dip in butter, then in cracker crumbs.

Place them on a greased cookie sheet; put in broiler, 4 inches from the flame. Cook 5 minutes; turn them over and cook 5 minutes longer. Serve hot.

COCONUT CANDIED SWEET POTATOES
(Top-of-the-Stove)

(2 Servings)

1 or 2 sweet potatoes,
   enough for 2 servings
1 tbsp. baking soda
   warm water to cover
½ cup sugar
½ cup water

a pinch of salt
a few pieces lemon or orange peel
¼ cup shredded coconut, optional
1 tbsp. butter

Peel potatoes and cut in diagonal chunks. Sprinkle soda over them and pour warm water to cover. Let them in soak in solution 5 minutes. Drain in colander.

In a saucepan that covers, add sweet potatoes, sugar, water, lemon and salt; boil, cover, cook over medium heat 10 minutes, uncover then cook 10 minutes longer. Add butter and coconut.

*FUN COOKING GUIDE: For a different treat, and to substitute coconut, may use any of the following; nutmeg, pineapple, walnuts, pecans, raisins, apple chunks or just serve plain. If using apples, cook even with the potatoes.

SWEET POTATO SURPRISE

1½ cups cooked mashed
   sweet potatoes
1 tablespoon. melted butter
¼ teaspoon salt
¼ teaspoon nutmeg or
   cinnamon

2 tablespoons raisins or
   (surprise) pecans, pineapple,
   drained, or coconuts
1 or 2 marshmallows, cut in 4
Post Toasties or cornflakes

In a bowl, combine sweet potatoes, salt, spices, butter and raisins; mix well. Divide mixture into 4 or more portions. Make indentation in center of each croquette. Place a piece of marshmallow in center; close partially (leave open a bit at top); toss in flakes, being careful not to squash. Place on baking sheet; bake in 350° (pre heated) oven for 15 or 20 minutes.

*FUN COOKING GUIDE: Can make surprises ahead of time and keep in refrigerator until mealtime; double up for a company treat.

YAM-PINEAPPLE DELIGHT

1½ cups Louisiana yams
   (boiled, peeled and mashed;
   fresh: or canned)
1 tablespoon melted butter
5 or 6 marshmallows, cut in half

pinch of salt
few dashes of nutmeg
½ cup crushed pineapple; drain
   off the liquid (not to be used)

Preheat oven to 400°. Combine yams, salt, butter and nutmeg; mix well. Place in a greased baking dish. Spread crushed pineapple over yam mixture. Bake 20 minutes. Place the cut marshmallows over baked yams and pineapple. Bake 5 minutes longer.

*FUN COOKING GUIDE: For a different taste treat, use raisins or nuts instead of the pineapple, then dot with marshmallows.

❖ Soups ❖

CREAM OF CARROT SOUP

Cook enough carrots to measure	2 cups milk
1 cup when mashed	2 cups chicken stock
3 tablespoons butter	salt and pepper to taste
2 tablespoons flour	chopped parsley

Melt butter in a heavy-bottomed saucepan. Add flour and stir until well blended. Gradually add milk and stir constantly until thick. Add carrots and broth. Season to taste. Serve hot, sprinkled with parsley.

*FUN COOKING GUIDE: If there is too much for your 2 servings, chill, then freeze.

BEET CONSOMMÉ

Drain juice from a large can of sliced beets and put juice in a deep saucepan.	1 medium onion, chopped
	salt and pepper to taste
	chives, chopped
Mash beets fine	½ cup sour cream
3 cups chicken stock	(commercial kind)
1½ tablespoons vinegar	2 whole cloves

In the saucepan with beet juice, add chicken stock, cloves, vinegar, onion, beets, salt and pepper. Boil 20 minutes. Serve in bouillon cups with a bit of sour cream and sprinkled with chives.

FRENCH ONION SOUP

2 large white onions, sliced fine	1 pint rich soup stock, beef or chicken
2 tablespoons butter	salt and pepper to taste

Sauté onions in butter until light brown, stirring constantly. Add soup stock and simmer half an hour. Season to taste. Serve with toast.

FARA'S ITALIAN LENTIL SOUP

¾ cup lentil peas
1 quart water
½ teaspoon salt
¼ cup olive oil
1 medium onion, chopped
1 clove garlic, minced

½ teaspoon oregano powder
1 sprig parsley, minced
¼ cup vermicelli, break in small
    pieces, and cook according to
    directions on package, drain
    and set aside

Wash peas in 3 or 4 waters and put in a saucepan with the water. Boil 30 minutes.

In a separate saucepan, sauté onions and garlic in olive oil until tender. Add to peas. Also add sugar and oregano. Cover and simmer. Add more water if needed.

EMERALD GREEN PEA SOUP

¾ cup dried green split peas
1 quart water
½ cup diced cooked ham
1 tablespoon cooking oil

1 small onion, chopped
small pinch nutmeg
small pinch cloves
salt and. pepper to taste

Wash peas in many waters; use a colander to drain.

Put peas with water in a deep saucepan having a tight-fitting cover. Cover and bring to a boil; then reduce heat to simmer. Cook 1 hour.

In the meantime, cook onion and ham in oil 5 minutes, stirring constantly. Add to peas; salt and pepper to taste and add spices.

Cook about 30 minutes longer. Serve hot.

❖ Salads ❖

CANDLESTICK SALAD

2 crisp lettuce leaves
2 large pineapple halves
  chill separately
1 banana, cut in half
2 maraschino cherries

2 teaspoon mayonnaise
  or salad dressing
2 tablespoons grated
  American cheese

When dinner is almost ready, place a lettuce leaf on a saucer with a slice of pineapple. In the hole in the center of the pineapple slice stand the cut half of banana. Even off upper end. Pour ¼ teaspoon mayonnaise on tip and sprinkle with cheese. Place red cherry on tip of banana, using a toothpick to hold cherry in place. The result should resemble a burning candle; and may be used for any festive occasion.

*FUN COOKING GUIDE: Lettuce will keep longer; if, when leaves are needed, do not cut with a knife, but break off leaves as needed. Keep remaining head in a plastic bag in vegetable pan of refrigerator. Lettuce will stay crisp.

RIPE OLIVE HOT SLAW

½ cup finely shredded cabbage
1 pimiento, finely chopped
¼ cup ripe olives
3 tablespoons salad oil
¼ prepared mustard
1 teaspoon sugar
yolk of 1 egg, well beaten

2 tablespoons water
½ teaspoon prepared
  horseradish
3 tablespoons vinegar
1 tablespoon evaporated milk
paprika
salt and pepper

In a saucepan, blend oil, vinegar, horseradish, water, mustard and sugar. Heat to boiling point. Slowly add mixture over egg and milk.

Return to heat and cook 1or 2 minutes, stirring constantly. Pour over cabbage, olives and pimiento, season with salt, pepper and paprika.

*FUN COOKING GUIDE: This salad is delicious served with an outside Bar-B-Q. Wrap shredded cabbage in a damp cloth and chill in refrigerator until salad is ready to serve. It will have added crispness.

APPLE AND RAISIN SALAD

1 medium apple, peeled and
cut into small pieces
1 stick celery, cut in small
pieces

¼ cup seedless raisins
2 tablespoons mayonnaise or
salad dressing

Combine all ingredients in a mixing bowl. Chill about 1 hour. Serve on let-tuce leaf.

*FUN COOKING GUIDE: For a different taste treat, add grated raw carrots.

RED BEAN SALAD

1 cup cooked red beans,
rinsed and drained
small piece sweet pickle
chopped fine
1 tablespoon minced onion,
chopped fine

2 teaspoons, capers
¼ teaspoon prepared mustard
2 tablespoons salad dressing
or mayonnaise
salt and pepper to taste
1 hard boiled egg, minced

In a bowl, combine beans, pickles, capers, mustard, onion and salad dress-ing. Mix well. Season to taste. Chill. Make two servings on lettuce leaves. Garnish with eggs and lemon wedge.

SERVING CANTALOUPE

A Southern hostess was given an extra tip by a restaurant chef. When the seeds are removed from cantaloupe, sprinkle evenly with a dusting of sugar and allow to stand until ready to serve. By the time the guests eat the can-taloupe, the sugar has been absorbed into the flesh of the fruit and the result is delicious.

FRUIT COMBINATIONS

Grapefruit sections with fresh strawberries
Orange and grapefruit sections with canned fruit
Orange sections with pineapple chunks
Orange sections with strawberries
Orange sections with banana slices chilled in orange juice
Orange sections with green or purple grapes

(Any of the above combinations can be used by making a compote or served on lettuce with your favorite dressing.)

Chunks of pineapple
Stuffed pear halves with
    cream cheese
Stuffed peach halves
Glazed apple wedges

stuffed prunes with pink
    cream cheese
Spiced crab apple
Cluster of frosted grapes
Radish flowers
Kumquats

(Select any of the above for salad or compote. They are very colorful for centerpiece and buffets.)

PINEAPPLE CHUNKS WITH SOUR CREAM

1 cup pineapple chunks
1 cup sour cream

dash of nutmeg

Combine pineapple chunks with sour cream. Chill before serving.

ORANGE AND COCONUT COMPOTE

2 medium sized oranges,
    peeled and cut in small
    pieces

¼ cup shredded coconut
3 tablespoons powdered sugar

Combine all in a bowl and chill 1 hour or longer.

CARROT AND COCONUT HEALTH SALAD

½ cup raw, grated carrots
3 tablespoons grated coconut
    (reserve 1 tablespoon for
    topping)
2 teaspoons Maraschino cherries
    or pineapple juice

1 teaspoon lemon juice
salad dressing or mayonnaise
    enough to moisten

Combine carrots, coconut, lemon juice and dressing. Mix well and chill. Serve on 2 lettuce leaves, sprinkle with remaining coconut and top with cherry or pineapple juice.

PINEAPPLE SLICES STUFFED WITH GRAPE CREAM CHEESE

2 large or 4 small slices
   pineapple
½ of 3 ounce package cream
   cheese

1½ tablespoon pure grape juice
½ teaspoon sugar

Beat the cream cheese and gradually add the sugar and grape juice. Beat with a spoon until creamy. Spoon the mixture in hollow of pineapple slice. Chill. Serve on a lettuce leaf. Mayonnaise may be used as a topping if desired.

*FUN COOKING GUIDE: This cream cheese filling is fine served on Bartlett pear salad.

PEAR AND GRAPE SALAD ON LETTUCE

4 pear halves
green or red grapes
2 tablespoons cream cheese

1 teaspoon salad dressing
lettuce

Soften cream cheese with dressing. Place pear halves on lettuce and spoon cheese dressing in cavity of pears. Place a few grapes over all.

SPICED STUFFED PRUNES AND APRICOTS

Cook prunes with clove and cinnamon stick in water to cover. Chill many hours. Stuff with cream cheese. Serve with apricots or orange sections with your favorite dressing.

PINEAPPLE SLAW

(2 Servings)

½ cup finely shredded cabbage
3 tablespoons crushed
   pineapple
½ apple, cut in small pieces
   (do not peel)

1 tablespoon fresh lemon juice
2 tablespoons salad dressing
few dashes salt

Wrap cabbage in a damp cloth in refrigerator until salad is ready to be served. Combine all remaining ingredients and mix well. Chill. When ready to serve, mix cabbage and pineapple mixture just before serving.

*FUN COOKING GUIDE: For a different taste treat, use green seedless grapes instead of pineapple.

GRAPE AND CABBAGE SALAD

(2 Servings)

³/₄ cup finely shredded cabbage
2 tablespoons salad dressing
   or mayonnaise

1 tablespoon apple cider vinegar
¼ cup green seedless grapes

Chill cabbage separately until ready to serve. Combine all ingredients and serve.

HOT POTATO SALAD

2 medium red potatoes, boiled in the skins in plenty of salted water 30 minutes.

DRESSING FOR SALAD

2 tablespoons salad oil
1 small onion, sliced fine
¼ teaspoon prepared mustard
¼ teaspoon sugar
a small piece celery, chopped

½ teaspoon capers
1 hard boiled egg, chopped fine
½ teaspoon chopped parsley
salt and pepper to taste

Peel potatoes while still hot. Slice thin and put in a salad dish. Season with salt and pepper. Cook onion in oil two or three minutes and while still crisp, add sugar, mustard, capers, egg, parsley and heat through. Pour mixture over potatoes. Good served hot.

GERMAN POTATO SALAD

Follow Hot Potato Salad recipe but instead of salad oil use bacon grease. Fry three slices bacon crisp and crumble over salad.

DILL SOUR GREEN BEANS

½ pound fresh green beans   1 pint salted boiling water

Wash, snap ends off beans and add to boiling water. Cook, stirring almost constantly 12 to 15 minutes until beans are tender crisp, but not soft. Drain off liquid. Add to sauce.

SAUCE:

1 tablespoon butter   pinch of dill seeds
1 teaspoon flour   1 small onion, sliced thin
½ cup sour cream
  (commercial kind)

Cook onion in butter 2 or 3 minutes. Stir in flour. When smooth, blend in cream and cook until thick and bubbly. Salt and pepper to taste. Combine with green beans and dill seeds.

*FUN COOKING GUIDE: This sauce is extra good on brussel sprouts, broccoli, asparagus or cauliflower.

MARINATED GREEN BEANS

½ pound green beans. Wash and break off ends. Break beans in small pieces. Boil in salted water until tender. Drain off liquid.

SAUCE FOR BEANS:

2 tablespoons vinegar   1 small onion, sliced
  (apple cider is fine)   (separate onion rings)
1 tablespoon salad oil   ½ clove garlic, mashed in
1 tablespoon chopped dill   ¼ teaspoon salt
  pickles   ½ teaspoon sugar

MARINATED GREEN BEANS
(Dressing for beans)

½ pound green beans cooked   2 tablespoons olive oil or
  as above   salad oil
½ clove garlic mashed in   2 tablespoons fresh lemon juice
¼ teaspoon salt   or apple cider vinegar
½ teaspoon sugar

Combine all the ingredients and mix well. Toss green beans in the dressing. Cover and chill hours before serving.

*FUN COOKING GUIDE: This dressing can also be used on other boiled vegetables, such as white squash, carrots, or beets.

LIME AND FRUIT JELL-O

½ package or 4 tablespoons
  lime Jell-O
1 cup hot water and fruit
  juice mixed

½ cup canned fruit cocktail or
  any fresh fruit; drain off
  liquid

(Make Jell-O hours before serving)

Pour boiling water over Jell-O. Mix well until dissolved. Chill. When consistency of egg white, add fruit. Chill until firm.

*FUN COOKING GUIDE: If I'm going to need only 2 or 3 servings, I only use half a package for fear of tiring of this dish.

CABBAGE BEET RELISH

1½ cups finely shredded
  cabbage
1 cup cooked beets, cut
  n strips
⅔ cup apple cider vinegar

⅓ cup sugar
¼ teaspoon salt
few dashes nutmeg
few dashes pepper
2 tablespoons horseradish

Combine cabbage, beets and horseradish.

Put remaining ingredients in a saucepan. Heat through and dissolve sugar. Pour over mixture of vegetables. Let stand several hours.

Can keep 2 or 3 days; flavor will improve.

*FUN COOKING GUIDE: This relish is a good companion to Bar-B-Q cookouts.

PICKLED BEETS

1 large can beets	1 cinnamon stick
½ cup beet juice	3 whole cloves
⅓ cup vinegar	½ teaspoon salt
¼ cup sugar	

Drain beets and put in a jar. Heat vinegar, beet juices, sugar, salt, cinnamon stick and cloves. Simmer, stirring to melt sugar. Pour over beets and seal. Chill.

*FUN COOKING GUIDE: The pickled beets will keep in the refrigerator for as long as two weeks.

PICKLED BABY OKRA

16 to 20 very small okra pods; washed. (Cut off both ends)

Cook in plenty of salted boiling water 15 minutes or until tender Do not overcook. Drain in colander.

PICKLING DRESSING:

4 tablespoons apple cider vinegar	1½ teaspoons salad oil
	salt and pepper to taste
2 tablespoons sweet pickle vinegar	slices from 1 large onion (do not peel until after
¼ teaspoon celery salt then separate slices.)	slices are cut ¼ inch thick

Combine all and add to okra. Let marinate at room temperature 1 or 2 hours before serving.

PICKLED CARROTS

2 or 3 carrots

Wash carrots well, then cook in plenty of salted water 20 minutes or until just tender. Do not overcook. Peel or skin off peeling while still warm; cut into long, finger-type strips. Make pickling dressing as one used for okra.

PICKLED WHITE SUMMER SQUASH

Use the young white squash, cut in large serving pieces. Boil plenty of salted water 15 or 20 minutes or until just tender. Do not overcook.

Marinate at room temperature in pickling dressing.

*FUN COOKING GUIDE: For a colorful and tasty salad, make mixture of beets, carrots, okra, pink onion rings, fresh sliced tomato and bell peppers.

PURPLE PICKLED EGGS

12 eggs, boiled 20 minutes and peeled	2 teaspoons mixed pickling spice
½ cup beet juice	1 large onion, cut ¼ inch
2 cups white vinegar	slices then peeled and
½ teaspoon salt	separated to make rings
1 teaspoon sugar cut in four	2 cloves garlic, peeled and

Combine vinegar, beet juice, salt, sugar and spice in a saucepan. Simmer 5 minutes. Place egg, garlic and onion in a large jar bowl and pour heated mixture over them. Chill.

*FUN COOKING GUIDE: These eggs can be kept as long as a week and are beautiful and decorative served with a meal, as a salad, for a buffet, picnic, or Bar-B-Q.

PINK ONION RINGS

Slice a large white onion ¼ inch thick. Push rings out to make individual rings. Peel last ring. Soak them a few minutes in canned beet juice. For added crispness, put in a plastic bag and chill before serving.

*FUN COOKING GUIDE: Pink onion rings are pretty as a garnish for meat, fish or vegetable dishes.

PINK ONION RINGS, ORANGE SLICES AND GREEN GRAPES

Make pink onion rings. Arrange onion rings, orange wedges and green grapes on lettuce leaves. Serve with favorite dressing or sour cream.

*FUN COOKING GUIDE: For an unusual combination serve chilled cantaloupe and watermelon balls, using a melon ball cutter to cut out balls; garnish with a sprig or two of mint.

MARINATED CUCUMBER SLICES

1 medium-sized cucumber unpaired and sliced thin. Add salt, pepper, oil and vinegar over cucumber. Let stand at room temperature.

BEETS IN ORANGE SAUCE

1 cup sliced beets	1 teaspoon corn starch
½ cup orange juice	pinch of salt
1 tablespoon sugar	

Combine orange juice, sugar, cornstarch, and salt in a saucepan. Cook and stir until sauce thickens. Add beets, heat through, and serve.

COUNTRY-STYLE BEETS AND POTATO SALAD

(6 Servings)

1 bunch fresh beets (boil in plenty of water 1 hour or until tender)	1 white onion sliced thin
	salt and black pepper
	4 tablespoons salad oil
3 new potatoes, boiled with skin until tender	2 teaspoon sugar
	3 tablespoons vinegar
2 hard boiled eggs	½ teaspoon prepared mustard

Peel and slice thin the potatoes, on a long platter sprinkle with salt and pepper. Over this, slice peeled beets very thin; salt and pepper lightly. Slice onion over all. Then slice the eggs.

Combine vinegar, oil, mustard, sugar, salt and pepper; in a saucepan, heat through, blend well, then pour mixture over all the vegetables.

*FUN COOKING GUIDE: This salad is a good companion to a summer Bar-B-Q cookout.

❖ *Dressings* ❖

ACADIAN ITALIAN SALAD DRESSING

Fill pint jar with:

5 or more cloves of garlic, mash;
  (do not use powdered garlic)
½ cup or more thinly sliced celery,
  may use celery leaves
½ cup or more thinly sliced bell
  pepper

⅓ cup or more thinly cut olives
  use your choice of green, black
  or stuffed olives

Fill the jar with your favorite salad oil. Choice of safflower, olive, corn or peanut oil. Mix all of the ingredients. Store in refrigerator. Will keep for weeks.

*FUN COOKING GUIDE: When using dressing on salad, COAT, but do not SOAK the vegetable with dressing. Sprinkle ghost of a shadow of sugar over all then use apple cider vinegar or lemon juice, home made bean sprouts, capers or poppy seed, then enjoy.

SALAD BOWL

For tender crispness, tear lettuce (do not cut), hours before using. Wrap in a damp towel. Use your favorite raw vegetable. Coat lightly with dressing, ghost of a shadow of sugar, then add a little vinegar, then enjoy. Dressing may be used on boiled cabbage, squash, broccoli, cauliflower, beets, carrots, green beans, okra or turnips.

*FUN COOKING GUIDE: Always add the vegetable to rapidly salted boiling water, cook until tender and crisp, 12 to 15 minutes. Whole beets should cook in 45 minutes.

TARTAR SAUCE

1 cup mayonnaise
1 tablespoon minced onion,
  or shallots
1 tablespoon capers
1 teaspoon vinegar

1 tablespoon chopped
  sweet pickles
½ teaspoon prepared mustard
1 hard boiled egg, chopped fine

Combine all ingredients and mix well. Chill in covered dish until ready to use. Serve with almost any fried fish.

*FUN COOKING GUIDE: If there is any leftover tartar sauce, it can be used on a salad.

FRENCH DRESSING FOR FRUIT SALAD

In a bowl, sift together the following ingredients:

½ cup granulated sugar
1 teaspoon paprika
1 teaspoon celery salt

1 teaspoon onion salt
1 teaspoon dry mustard
1 teaspoon salt

Add the following ingredients alternately to dry ingredients. Dressing will thicken. Add last addition of vinegar as dressing thickens.

1 cup salad oil
¼ cup apple cider vinegar

lastly, add 1 or 2 drops of red
  food coloring

*FUN COOKING GUIDE: Use this dressing on fruit, molded salads, grapefruit, melon salads. If dressing should separate on standing, beat well.

THOUSAND ISLAND DRESSING

½ cup mayonnaise
¼ cup catsup
Piece green pepper, chopped
1 hard boiled egg

2 tablespoons chili sauce
1 gherkin, chopped
2 tablespoons onion, chopped
A dash of Tabasco sauce

Combine all ingredients and mix thoroughly. Chill before serving. Especially good on wedge of heart of lettuce.

*FUN COOKING GUIDE: For added crispness, never cut lettuce with a knife, but break off if only using leaves. Chill in a damp cloth.

*FUN COOKING GUIDE: Never, never, never wet or wash any vegetable before putting in vegetable crisper. Celery or any vegetable will keep indefinitely.

SWEET AND HOT CHOW CHOW
(Makes about 3½ pints)

3 cups diced cucumber
(about 3)
1½ cups shredded cabbage
1½ cups chopped onions

1 cup chopped green tomatoes
(3 or 4)
½ cup chopped green peppers
½ cup chopped celery

Put vegetables in a large bowl; pour ⅓ cup salt over all. Mix well and let stand for 4 hours. Drain, rinse well. Pour water to cover, add one teaspoon powdered alum. Keep in refrigerator for 1 hour. Drain. Make sauce.

SAUCE

2 cups vinegar
⅓ cup flour
¾ cup sugar
¾ cup prepared mustard
½ teaspoon salt
½ teaspoon red pepper

1 teaspoon turmeric powder
1 pinch clove
1 pinch allspice
1 pinch cinnamon
1 pinch nutmeg
¼ cup oil

Heat 2 cups vinegar in a large saucepan. Combine flour, sugar, pepper, turmeric, salt and spices. Mix well, gradually stir in mustard. Then remaining ¾ cup vinegar, stir carefully not to have lumps. Stir mixture into heated vinegar, cook about 5 minutes or until sauce thickens. Add drained vegetables and oil. Cook until mixture comes to a hard boil. Pack in sterilized jars.

*FUN COOKING GUIDE: **Canned Tomatoes for Salads or cocktails** - I don't like force ripened or fresh tomatoes, so I use vine-ripen canned tomatoes, which are much more delicious.

*FUN COOKING GUIDE: **Dry Hands** - If there is any dampness at all on your hands, the garlic will spoil, such as soften, darken, or rot. It is wise to separate a few cloves in a small plastic bag or in a vegetable crisper.

❖ Breads ❖

APPLE FRITTERS

1 cooking apple,
  medium sized
²/₃ cup flour
½ teaspoon salt
1 teaspoon baking powder
⅓ cup milk

half eggshell of beaten egg
2 tablespoons brown sugar
3 tablespoons of either wine,
  rum, brandy or lemon
  juice (your choice)

In a mixing bowl, combine sugar and wine. Stir until sugar is dissolved. Peel apple and slice thin slices into mixture. Let stand 1 hour or longer, stirring occasionally to coat apples. Make a batter by combining flour, salt, baking powder, milk and egg. Beat until smooth. Let rest at room temperature one hour and cover with a cloth. When ready to fry, add apples; drained. Heat cooking oil in a small skillet. Oil should be about 1½ inches deep. Use a tablespoon to drop into hot oil. Dip into oil each time so batter won't stick to spoon. Fry a minute or two. With a slotted spoon take out on paper. Sprinkle with powdered sugar.

*FUN COOKING GUIDE: Can also use thick slices of bananas in batter; cut only when ready to fry. Use for desert, coffee or T.V. snacks.

BANANA NUT BREAD

2 cups flour
2 tsps. baking powder
¼ tsp. salt
¼ cup butter or margarine
²/₃ cup sugar
2 well beaten eggs

1½ cups very ripe bananas,
  mashed
¾ cups nuts, chopped
  pecans or walnuts
¼ cup milk
¼ tsp. baking soda

Sift together, flour, baking powder, soda and salt, set aside. Beat butter and sugar until creamy, add sugar and continue beating until light and creamy, add eggs, banana and milk, beat well; add flour mixture, beat until smooth, fold in nuts. Turn into a well greased bread pan (8½ x 4½ x 3) and bake in a moderate preheated oven (350 degrees) for 1 hour. Cook on a rack.

*FUN COOKING GUIDE: Very ripe bananas can be purchased cheaper, look for the bargain.

*FUN COOKING GUIDE: Store well wrapped until next day; or chill and freeze until day of a party. May make into finger cherry cheese sandwiches.

CHEESE CHERRY FILLING

Soften two 3-ounce packages of cream cheese with maraschino cherry juice until spread consistency. Add finely chopped cherries. Cut banana nut bread into ¼ inch slices; spread with whipped butter, then with cherry cheese mixture, then put slices together, wrap and chill, sandwich fashion. Cut each sandwich in three, finger fashion. Serve on platter lined with a pretty paper doily.

*FUN COOKING GUIDE: After they are cut, may be placed in a wax paper lined box and frozen.

BREADS

Cut French bread in 1 inch slices, but do not cut through. Leave part of the bottom unsliced. Allow each person to break off as needed.

*FUN COOKING GUIDE: These breads are good companions for outside Bar-B-Q's or fish fries.

HERB BREAD

½ pound butter
3 tablespoons chopped parsley
3 tablespoons green onion tops
2 tablespoons milk

¼ cup finely shredded celery
  leaves
1 teaspoon sweet basil or
  rosemary

Cream or whip butter well. Add remaining ingredients. Spread the butter mixture between slices of bread. Wrap bread in aluminum foil and put in refrigerator 24 hours. Heat 20 to 25 minutes 350° oven.

CELERY BREAD

Combine well-whipped butter (½ cup) with ¼ teaspoon salt, ½ teaspoon celery seed, ¼ teaspoon paprika and ¼ teaspoon red pepper. Spread between slices of French bread. Keep wrapped in foil. Chill. When ready to use heat in preheated oven, 325° for 20 minutes.

GARLIC BREAD

½ cup whipped butter
2 cloves garlic, mashed
 Paprika

¼ cup Parmesan cheese
¼ teaspoon salt

Combine all ingredients except cheese and paprika. Cover and let stand at room temperature 30 minutes or longer for flavor to permeate the butter. Cut loaf in diagonal slices, being careful not to cut through. Spread the butter, then sprinkle with cheese and paprika. Wrap in foil. Bake in 325° preheated oven 15 minutes.

Break as desired.

BEST-EVER CORN BREAD

1¼ cup cornmeal
¾ cup boiling water
1 teaspoon salt
2 teaspoons sugar
3 teaspoons baking powder
1 well beaten egg

2 tablespoons melted butter or
 cooking oil
¼ cup all-purpose flour
¼ cup evaporated milk
¼ cup water

Pour boiling water over cornmeal; stir well and set aside to cool. Combine cornmeal mixture and with all remaining ingredients, beat until well blended; let rest a while - improves texture.

Preheat over 400°; pour butter into a greased square pan or muffin pan, bake about 20 minutes.

*FUN COOKING GUIDE: This cornbread recipe will make 4 or 5 good servings. Add 1 tablespoon cooking oil in a heavy bottom skillet; pour about half the mixture in heated skillet; cover on top of the stove over very low heat 10 minutes then turn over with spatula and cook 10 minutes longer. The remaining batter can be kept for as long as 2 or 3 days in a covered dish; flavor will improve, also texture.

PEPPERED CORN SPOON BREAD

½ cup yellow cornmeal
1 cup cream style corn
⅔ cup buttermilk mixed with
½ teaspoon soda
1 teaspoon baking powder
1 teaspoon salt
1 egg yolk

1 egg white, beat until stiff
⅔ cup grated American cheese or
Cheddar
1 small onion, chopped fine
2 jalapeño peppers, chopped fine
and a little juice
¼ cup salad oil

Preheat oven to 400°.

Cook onion in salad oil until tender. Combine cornmeal, salt and baking powder, add corn, then onion mixture and remaining ingredients except egg white. Fold in stiffly beaten egg whites last. Pour into a 1 quart baking dish. Bake 25 or 30 minutes.

*FUN COOKING GUIDE: This cornbread is a good companion to choice of boiled cabbage, greens, or any cooked dry beans.

*FUN COOKING GUIDE: Grate all the chunks of cheese over a piece of wax paper on a cookie sheet, freeze for about 1 hour. Pour in a plastic bag and keep frozen until ready to use. Keeps a long time. Will not mold.

PEPPERED CORN BREAD

Same ingredients used as Peppered Corn Spoon Bread above only egg yolk and white is beaten together. Pour batter into a greased pan. Bake in 400° preheated oven 20 minutes.

QUICK BREAD PUFFS

1 cup all-purpose flour
2 teaspoons baking powder
½ teaspoon salt

1 teaspoon sugar
½ cup plus 1 tablespoon milk

Combine all ingredients and beat batter well. Heat cooking oil, 1 inch deep in a frying pan; drop by teaspoonful in very hot oil and fry brown. Take up on paper toweling.

*FUN COOKING GUIDE: These little puffs are very inexpensive to make and be served with dinner, or breakfast; also makes a good T.V. snack served with jelly, jam or Louisiana cane syrup.

FRITTERS
They are called Beignet (Ban Yay) in French

1 cup all-purpose flour
2 teaspoons baking powder
½ teaspoon salt

½ cup milk
1 well beaten egg

Combine egg and milk, gradually add flour, baking powder and salt

Beat well. Drop by teaspoon into 2 inches of hot oil, fry brown. Drain on paper toweling. Makes approximately 2 dozen fritters. Serve with jam, jelly or syrup.

*FUN COOKING GUIDE: For the sake of your health - use wheat germ, whole wheat four or bran flour to make 1 cup.

CUSH-CUSH

¼ cup cooking oil
1 cup yellow or white corn meal
3 tablespoons all-purpose flour
1 teaspoon baking powder
½ teaspoon salt

2 teaspoons sugar
⅔ cup water
¼ cup milk
1 tablespoon butter

Combine corn meal, flour, baking powder, salt and sugar, mix well, gradually add water.

In a heavy bottom pot, add oil and corn meal mixture, cover with a tight-fitting lid and place over medium heat; cook 5 minutes. Uncover and stir, cover, cook again, reduce heat to low, cook 15 minutes longer stirring occasionally; then add milk and butter. Cover for a minute or two.

Serve hot with Louisiana cane syrup, or as a cereal with milk.

*FUN COOKING GUIDE: This dish originated from the Indians and passed on to the Acadians and is a delicious health giving food.

CORN DODGERS

1 cup Cornmeal
½ teaspoon salt

1 cup boiling water
cooking oil to fry

In a bowl combine cornmeal and salt. Add the boiling water, stir until all the lumps are gone. Cover tightly for about 5 or 10 minutes. This will swell the meal. Heat oil, pat portions between your hands to make an oblong cake ¼ inch thick. Fry on both sides until golden.

*FUN COOKING GUIDE: These corn cakes are delicious for a snack or good companion to beans or vegetables, especially boiled cabbage.

❖ Desserts ❖

FESTIVE TIPSY PUDDING
My Award Winner

(6 servings)

3 cups milk
¼ cup raw rice
½ teaspoon salt
3 egg yolks
3 egg whites
½ cup sugar
⅓ cup drained maraschino
   cherries, chopped

2 tablespoons sugar for
   meringue
1 teaspoon fresh lemon juice
   for meringue
1 teaspoon vanilla
¼ teaspoon nutmeg (fresh
   grated is best)

Combine milk, rice and salt in a small saucepan that covers. Cook over high heat, when it comes to a hard boil reduce heat very low. Cover and cook ten minutes. (Do not peep). Let stand another ten minutes. Cool.

Beat egg yolks until creamy, add sugar, beat until granules disappear. Add vanilla, cherries, and rice mixture. Mix well. Pour into a well buttered baking dish. Bake in preheated oven 350° for 30 minutes. While pudding is baking, beat egg whites until very stiff and forms a peak; not until then, add sugar and lemon juice. Pile high in servings on pudding. Bake two or three minutes longer. Serve with "Tipsy Sauce" poured over each serving.

TIPSY SAUCE

Rinse pan thoroughly, so milk won't scorch. Heat 1 cup milk. Combine 1 ½ tablespoons sugar and 2 teaspoons cornstarch; add to milk, cook over low heat until thick and smooth - about three minutes. Cool. Add a jigger of brandy (optional) and a few chopped cherries. Top each serving of pudding with sauce.

*FUN COOKING GUIDE: Make sauce pink by adding 1 or 2 drops of red food coloring.

EASTER EGG SQUARES

3 egg whites
1 cup sifted confectioners sugar
½ cup butter
¾ cup sugar
¼ teaspoon salt and
3 egg yolks

⅓ cup lemon juice
1 tablespoon orange rind
½ cup pecan or walnuts
1¼ cup flour, sifted with
½ teaspoon baking powder

Preheat oven 375°

Cream butter with the ¾ cups sugar until fluffy. Add egg yolks, one at a time, creaming well each time. Gradually add sifted flour mixture.

Beat egg whites until stiff, gradually add confectioners sugar and lemon juice, alternately, creaming well each time. Fold pecans and orange rind into egg whites and fold into sugar and flour mixture. Pour into a well-greased 13 x 9 x 2 inch pan. Bake 25 minutes. Frost while still lukewarm. Cut in squares. Place halves of small jelly beans, cut sidedown on squares.

EASTER EGG FROSTING:

3 ounces package cream, cheese
4 tablespoons crushed
pineapple or juice

⅛ teaspoon salt
2½ cups confectioners sugar

Soften the cream cheese with pineapple juice, mixing a little at a time. Add salt. Gradually add sugar and beat until creamy. Spread on cake.

*FUN COOKING GUIDE: These little cakes are good served for parties especially for children.

Use candy according to seasonal themes such a Valentine hearts, Mardi Gras, or Christmas.

COCONUT MOLD WITH BERRIES

(8 Servings)

2 tablespoons unflavored
    gelatin
½ cup milk
1½ cup milk
½ cup sugar

¼ teaspoon salt   .
½ pint whipping cream
2 cups coconut, fresh or
    canned
1 teaspoon vanilla

In a large bowl, dissolve gelatin in ½ cup milk. Set aside

Heat milk, salt and sugar. Mix well, Stir into gelatin mixture and put in refrigerator to chill until mixture thickens to consistency of egg white. With beater, beat until light and fluffy. Add vanilla.

Whip the heavy cream until stiff; fold into gelatin mixture, then fold in the coconut. Pour into a ring mold or any fancy mold and chill in refrigerator until firm. Unmold on pretty flat dish.

*FUN COOKING GUIDE: Serve with a choice of fresh raspberries, black berries, blue berries and or apricots or peaches.

*FUN COOKING GUIDE: If there is any leftover coconut mold it is delicious in any fruit flavor Jell-O.

APPLE SNOW

½ cup sugar	1 sour apple, grated
1 egg white	1 teaspoon lemon juice

In top of double boiler combine sugar, egg white and apple. Place double boiler over bottom part with boiling water. Cook over medium heat; beat mixture with egg beater until light and frothy.

Should be the consistency of marshmallow.

*FUN COOKING GUIDE: Don't ever stop beating; until frothy. Use as a topping for cakes, ice cream, or puddings.

PEACH COBBLER

Arrange 2 cups peaches in shallow baking dish. Use all the juice from the can, adding ¼ cup sugar, 1 tablespoon tapioca, 1 teaspoon grated lemon peel, 1 teaspoon lemon juice and 1 teaspoon almond extract. Heat in oven or on top of the stove.

Preheat oven 400°.

MAKE BATTER:

¾ cup flour	½ shell of beaten egg
1½ teaspoon baking powder	⅓ cup milk
½ teaspoon salt	1 tablespoon brown sugar
¼ cup soft butter	

Sift flour, baking powder and salt. With a fork cut the butter to size of small peas. Combine milk, sugar and egg. Add to flour mixture and beat well. Spoon over heated peaches. Bake 30 minutes.

*FUN COOKING GUIDE: If you are using fresh peaches, peel and slice to make 2 cups, 1½ cup water, ½ cup sugar and juice of half a lemon.

FRESH BERRY COBBLER

*FUN COOKING GUIDE: For fresh berry cobbler Heat about 2 cups fresh berries to ½ cup sugar and ½ cup water. Make batter as for peach cobbler and bake 30 minutes.

APPLE CRUNCH DELIGHT

(6 Servings)

Pare and slice 6 or 8 apples. Arrange in square pan or pie plate.

Mix together:

¾ **cups brown sugar**	¼ **cup butter**
¾ **cups all-purpose flour**	¾ **cup chopped nuts**
¼ **teaspoon salt**	**cinnamon**

Spread mixture over apples. Sprinkle with cinnamon. Bake 1 hour in a preheated 350° oven. Serve warm with whipped cream.

*FUN COOKING GUIDE: Now friends, this is the apple desert dish I have been keeping for this book.

FROZEN WHIPPED CREAMS

Many, Many Servings

½ **pint whipping cream**	**1 teaspoon vanilla**
1 tablespoon sugar	

With a beater whip cream stiffly. Add sugar and vanilla. Oil a cookie sheet; cover with a piece of wax paper. Drop cream by large tablespoonfuls. Place in freezer 3 or 4 hours, drop frozen cream in a large plastic bag; take out as needed.

*FUN COOKING GUIDE: These frozen whipped creams are especially good on apple pie, or any of favorite deserts.

BAKED CHEESE CAKE WITH BLUEBERRY TOPPING

In a spring cake pan, line bottom and sides with mixture of:

1¼ cup graham cracker crumbs	3 tablespoons sugar
⅓ cup melted butter	¼ teaspoon cinnamon

Mix well before lining and pack.

Preheat oven 350°.

CHEESE CAKE

½ pound cream cheese	¼ cup sugar
1 cup sour cream	2 drops almond extract
3 egg yolks	1 teaspoon lemon juice
3 egg whiles, stiffly beaten	½ teaspoon vanilla
¼ teaspoon salt	2 extra tablespoons sugar

Soften cheese, by adding sour cream a little at a time and stir until smooth. In a separate bowl, beat egg yolk until lemon colored; add sugar slowly, beating well; stir into cream cheese mixture, add vanilla, almond, and lemon juice. Beat egg whites stiff; add extra sugar. Beat until granules melt. Fold in stiffly beaten egg whites; mix well, then pour into graham cracker lined pan. Bake 1 hour; turn off heat and let cake stand in the oven 1 hour. Turn off heat, cool in oven. Pour 1 cup Blueberries pie filling over top. Chill before serving. May serve with whipped cream.

*FUN COOKING GUIDE: Any of the following glazed fruits can be substituted for topping; strawberries, cherries, raspberries, black berries, apricot, or peaches. Make glaze for fruit as following for blueberry topping. Use canned or fresh.

BLUEBERRY TOPPING

1 cup fresh or frozen blueberries	2 teaspoons lemon juice
	2 tablespoons sugar
½ cup water	1½ teaspoons cornstarch

Heat blueberries and water, blend sugar and cornstarch; add to blueberries. Cook and stir constantly until smooth, add lemon juice, chill. Pour over cheese cake.

ICEBOX PEACH CHEESE CAKE

Graham cracker crumb crust
   as above
1 package (8 oz.) cream cheese
½ cut sour cream

¼ cup sugar
1 teaspoon fresh lemon juice
1 teaspoon almond extract

Bake crust in a 375 ° preheated oven 8 or 10 minutes. Soften cream cheese; gradually add sugar and cream alternately; beat until fluffy after each addition; add lemon juice and almond; pour mixture into cooled crust; chill 2 or 3 hours before garnishing top of cake with peach glaze.

PEACH GLAZE

4 or 5 peach halves, canned
½ cup peach juice
1½ tablespoons sugar
1½ teaspoons cornstarch

1 teaspoon almond flavor
1 or 2 drops yellow food
   coloring
pinch of salt

Slice peaches thin and form 2 circles around cake.

In a saucepan blend sugar and cornstarch; add peach juice; cook over low heat, stirring constantly until thickened and smooth; remove from heat; add salt, almond and food coloring; cool. Pour over peaches; chill again before serving.

*FUN COOKING GUIDE: Can substitute with many other fruits; such as apricots, cherries, pineapple, strawberries, raspberries or blueberries.

BREAD PUDDING

(4 Good Servings)

2 slices, stale bread
2 cups milk
4 level tbsp. sugar
2 egg yolks
1 tsp. vanilla
¼ tsp. salt

a few dashes nutmeg
2 egg whites
2 extra tbsp. sugar
1 tbsp. lemon juice
butter

Preheat oven 350°.

In a bowl combine milk, bread, vanilla and salt. Soak a while.

In a separate bowl beat egg yolk and 4 tbsp. sugar until creamy. Add to milk mixture. Pour into a well buttered quart sized baking dish. Sprinkle with nutmeg. Bake about 25 minutes, or until a toothpick comes out clean.

While pudding is baking, beat egg white until stiff and frothy; add 2 tablespoons sugar and lemon juice.

Remove from oven and place meringue in 3 or 4 mounds. Put dish back in oven and bake 2 or 3 minutes more. Serve hot or cold.

*FUN COOKING GUIDE: For a different taste treat; top with sauces, such as chocolate, caramel or rum sauce.

*FUN COOKING GUIDE: Another taste treat. Coconut or raisins are very tasty, so add to pudding before baking.

CARAMEL OR BUTTERSCOTCH SAUCE

2 tablespoons sugar
¼ cup water
¼ cup evaporated milk
1 tablespoon sugar

1 level teaspoon cornstarch
1 teaspoon butter
½ teaspoon vanilla

In a saucepan over low heat, melt sugar and let brown, almost burn, then add water and milk, stirring almost constantly.

Mix cornstarch and remaining sugar and add to sauce, also add butter and vanilla, stir and cook until smooth. Chill and serve as a topping for pudding or ice cream.

*FUN COOKING GUIDE: Toast pecans to use over sauce.

HARD SAUCE

4 tablespoons butter
¾ cup fine sugar
juice of half a lemon
pinch of salt

½ teaspoon vanilla
1 tablespoon brandy
½ cup rich cream

Beat butter until smooth, adding sugar gradually. Add salt, vanilla and brandy and beat again. Add cream. Chill. Serve over plum pudding.

*FUN COOKING GUIDE: Also good served on spice cakes.

RUM SAUCE

(4 Servings)

⅓ cup evaporated milk
⅓ cup water
1½ tablespoons sugar
1 jigger rum

1½ teaspoon cornstarch
pinch of salt
half a teaspoon butter

Heat water and milk in a small saucepan; combine sugar, cornstarch and salt, stir into the heated milk until smooth; add butter; cool.

Then add rum. Serve on Pound Cake, Puddings or Ice Cream.

*FUN COOKING GUIDE: For a different taste treat use brandy.

CREAMY COCONUT PRALINES

3 cups sugar
¾ cup evaporated milk
1 tablespoon white corn syrup
¼ teaspoon salt

1 tablespoon butter
2 cups coconut
1 teaspoon vanilla

Combine sugar, milk, syrup, salt and butter in heavy bottom saucepan, preferably with a copper bottom or stainless steel. Cook over medium, then low heat, stirring almost constantly. Test a few drops in cold water to soft ball stages. Remove pot, let cool about 10 or 15 minutes. Add vanilla and coconut. Beat until glossy. Drop by tablespoonfuls on greased surface or waxed paper.

SOUTH LOUISIANA PRALINES

2 cups sugar
⅓ cup evaporated milk
1 tablespoon butter

⅛ teaspoon salt
1 teaspoon vanilla
1 cup toasted pecans
   (toast in 225° oven)

In a heavy bottom pot, add 1 tablespoon sugar, cook to a deep golden brown. Add about 1 tbsp. water, sugar, milk, butter and salt, stirring until it all comes to a boil. Cook about 15 minutes, test a few drops of the syrup in a little water, when two drops form a soft ball, roll around with your fingertips, water should be clear with no scum or film in view. Let cool to lukewarm.

Add pecans and vanilla, beat until glossy, drop by tablespoons on greased surface or wax paper. Should make about 30 pralines.

❖ *Lagniappe* ❖

THE WORD LAGNIAPPE was used by the Louisiana FRENCH when a merchant threw in a trifling gift for good measure.

RUM BALLS

Crushed vanilla wafers, crushed to measure 2 cups

1 cup finely chopped nuts,   **⅓ cup rum**
  (any kind)   **1 tablespoon white corn syrup**
2 tablespoons, melted butter   **1 tablespoon cocoa**

Combine all the ingredients, mix well and form into walnut sized balls and roll in powdered sugar. Store a week before using.

*FUN COOKING GUIDE: Can use day old cake instead of wafers. Also use whiskey or brandy instead of rum.

CORNICHON de MIRLITON
(French for Pickles of Vegetable Pears)

Peel mirliton and cut in finger sized lengths pack as many jars as you like. Pour apple cider vinegar in each jar (to measure vinegar needed) Pour vinegar into a saucepan, heat to boiling. Cut large chunks of onion, about 2 cloves garlic per jar, and long hot peppers, red or green and a little salt in each jar. Pour boiling vinegar in each jar and seal.

*FUN COOKING GUIDE: Other vegetables can be used such as turnips, green tomatoes, or cauliflower.

SOUR CREAM DRESSING FOR BAKED POTATOES

1 cup sour cream
⅓ cup chopped chives or
  green onions

1 tablespoon lemon juice
salt and white pepper to taste

Combine all, and serve with baked potatoes.

*FUN COOKING GUIDE: For a different taste treat fry three slices of bacon, crumble, and combine sour cream with bacon, ⅛ teaspoon garlic salt, lemon and 1 tablespoon sweet pickles.

REMOULADE SAUCE FOR SHRIMP

2 hard boiled egg yolks
1 raw egg yolk
1 teaspoon prepared mustard
1 teaspoon horseradish
¼ teaspoon salt

3 tablespoons tarragon vinegar
¼ cup apple cider vinegar
1 tablespoon parsley
1 tablespoon minced onion
½ cup salad oil

Blend egg yolks, salt, horseradish and mustard, beat thoroughly, add 2 teaspoon vinegar, beat a few minutes, next add 1 teaspoon oil, beating 2 or 3 minutes before adding the next, continue add vinegar and oil until all is used, then add parsley and onion. Pour remoulade over boiled peeled shrimp and let in a covered dish, many hours in refrigerator.

CHICKEN SPAGHETTI

1 large frying chicken, cut into
  serving pieces
1 teaspoon salt
½ teaspoon red pepper
1 medium onion, chopped
1 stick celery
2 cloves garlic, minced
1 small bell pepper, cut in
  small pieces

3 cups whole tomatoes, canned
1 can Italian tomato paste
1 teaspoon sugar
½ teaspoon sweet basil
1 piece bay leaf
1 tablespoon grated Romano
  cheese.

Season chicken with salt and pepper, heat cooking oil in a large heavy-bottomed pot, fry pieces of chicken a few at a time, do not crowd, brown but not done, take up on a platter. To the oil and drippings, add onion and celery, sauté for about 5 minutes, stirring constantly, then add Italian tomato paste, whole tomatoes chopped, garlic, bell pepper, sugar, sweet basil, bay leaf, cheese and about 2 cups water; when all the mixture comes to a boil reduce heat to simmer and cook 2 hours, stirring and add water when needed, add fried chicken and simmer 1 hour longer, season. Serve with cooked spaghetti.

*FUN COOKING GUIDE: Meatballs may be substituted for chicken.

SAUCE PIQUANTE

Louisiana version of tomato sauce made sharp and peppery. SO.

*FUN COOKING GUIDE: Make with choice of Rabbit, Squirrel, Deer meat, Turtle, Tripe, or Chicken; Make as above spaghetti sauce only add very much red pepper.

OYSTER SPAGHETTI, CAJUN STYLE

(2 Servings)

1-12 oz. jar fresh oysters, or
   2¹/₂ dozen
2 tablespoons cooking oil
2 tablespoons all-purpose flour
1 small onion, finely chopped
1 clove garlic, minced
¹/₂ cup whole tomatoes
2 tablespoons tomato paste or
   ¹/₄ cup tomato sauce

1 piece of bell pepper chopped
¹/₂ teaspoon sugar
1 cup water including liquid
   from cooked oysters
Salt and pepper to taste
¹/₄ pound spaghetti cooked in
   boiling water until tender

Place oysters in a saucepan and cook in their own liquid until edges begin to curl, and they will swell. Pour in colander, allowing all liquid to drain out, reserve oysters, add liquid to water.

In a heavy-bottomed pot heat oil, add flour, cook stirring constantly until a golden brown, add onion, cook until tender. Then add garlic, tomatoes, paste, bell pepper and water. Cook about 20 minutes, then add cooked spaghetti. Season to taste. Add oysters just before serving.

*FUN COOKING GUIDE: My Mom and all people the Louisiana way served spaghetti mixed in sauces. Our Italian friends serve it separately.

*FUN COOKING GUIDE: When I need tomato sauce and whole tomatoes canned, I usually buy the largest cans, use what I needed for recipe, then usually fill 2 ice cube trays, freeze then loosen tomato cubes into plastic bag. When frozen, use a few as needed. "Sure will save money".

SHRIMP JAMBALAYA
My Third Prize Winner in 1973 International Rice Festival

1 1b. shrimp, peel, devein and
  season with salt and pepper
2 tbsp. butter or margarine
⅛ cup cooking oil
2 tbsp. flour
1 cup chopped onion
½ cup chopped celery (may use
  leaves)
¾ cup whole tomatoes,
  cut in pieces

2 cloves garlic, minced
  very small piece of bay leaf
1½ cups rice
1 tsp. .salt
2½ cups of water
A little of each - chopped parsley,
  green onion and pimiento
Sliced lemon.
Red pepper to taste

In a heavy-bottomed pot, heat oil, add flour, cook and stir over medium heat until dark golden brown, add onion, cook until tender, add tomatoes, celery, garlic, bay leaf and 1 cup of water. Cook about 10 minutes, stir occasionally. Add rice, salt, red pepper and water; when it comes to a hard boil, reduce heat, cover with a tight-fitting lid. Cook 15 minutes. Do not peep. Let stand 15 minutes longer. In the meantime, melt butter, add seasoned shrimp. Cook stirring constantly for about 8 to 10 minutes. They should curl on edges and turn pink.

Stir into cooked rice. Let jambalaya stay covered a while to improve flavor. Then add parsley, green onion and pimiento. Serve with lemon wedges.

*FUN COOKING GUIDE: For an added taste treat, add a few oysters. Cook 2 minutes with shrimp.

MARGARET'S TWO-IN-ONE BAR-B-Q SAUCE

COOKING TIME - 30 minutes

APPROXIMATE COST-ABOUT 90¢ for 1½ quarts

3 cups cooking oil
4 cups onions (or 6 medium
  onions finely chopped)
1 14 oz. bottle catsup
2 teaspoons prepared mustard
⅓ cup Worcestershire sauce
1 tablespoon lemon juice, with
  1 tablespoon chopped lemon rind

1 tablespoon apple cider
  vinegar
½ teaspoon salt
3 tablespoon honey (this
  glazes chicken or meats)

Pour oil in a heavy saucepan, add chopped onions, and slowly cook for about 15 minutes, stirring occasionally, or until onions are nicely sautéed. Stir in 1 bottle catsup, simmer 5 minutes longer.

In a cup, combine mustard, Worcestershire sauce, lemon juice and rind, vinegar, salt and honey, and add to cooked onion mixture. Cook about 10 minutes longer.

*FUN COOKING GUIDE: Definition of two-in-one.

1. Set Bar-B-Q sauce aside until seasoned oil settles to the top (to be used for daubing chicken while barbecuing)

1. Settled onion sauce is to be eaten with garlic French bread.

ABBIES BAR-B-Q'D CHICKEN

Light charcoal, but do not start barbecuing until coals have burned for one half-hour because chicken must be cooked on slow fire. Coat chicken with above oil, and place on greased grill, turning chicken over every 15 or 20 minutes, each time daubing chicken with oil, and cook for approximately 2½ to 3 hours.

*FUN COOKING GUIDE: Abbie says use paper plates, etc, and above all, be yourself - Relax and have fun.

Hint—To make preparation of above sauce earlier and also for a hurry-up, neater cleanup job, gather all ingredients in a tray, place before you on left side of working area, and as you use one ingredient place on right side. This way, if there are any interruptions you will not forget which ingredient has already been used. Then place used ingredients back on tray and return to storage place.

ROUX

A ROUX is made in advance for sauces, gravies and gumbos.

1 cup cooking oil   **1 cup flour**

In a heavy-bottomed pot, add cooking oil, place over medium heat. Add flour, stir constantly until golden brown. This should take about 20 minutes. (But don't depend upon my timing.)

When roux is a rich, golden brown, take pot away from heat and continue stirring. When you think it is the right brown, hurry and dish it out into a permanent container. Reserve for future use. This roux will keep in refrigerator for weeks, even months.

FUN COOKING GUIDE: Always when adding to sauces, gravies or gumbos, there should be extra fat, cook onion until tender, add whatever ROUX is needed, then remaining ingredients to improve flavor, texture and color.

SAUCE TO DARKEN GRAVIES
(Soups, Gumbos or steak mushroom)

½ cup sugar   **1 cup water**

In a heavy-bottomed saucepan, over medium heat, add sugar. Cook until sugar melts then burns to a dark brown; shake pan but do not stir with spoon. Add water, cook until all the sugar is cooked into a syrup. Will store in refrigerator. Add a little to dishes as needed.

SEA FOOD AND OKRA GUMBO

(4 Servings)

½ pound shrimp. Peel and devein

4 serving pieces of fish (choice of red fish, cat fish or your favorite kind)

½ cup crab meat

1½ dozen oysters. Reserve liquid

¼ cup cooking oil

⅓ cup all purpose flour

1 medium size onion. Finely chopped

2 or 3 thin slices lemon

2 clove garlic, minced

3½ pints broth

1 cup whole tomatoes, fresh or canned, cut in pieces

½ pound okra, fresh or frozen, cut in small slices

1 bay leaf (optional)

salt and pepper to taste

1 tablespoon green onion, chopped

1 tablespoon parsley, chopped

Cook fish in salted water about 10 minutes. Drain off liquid and reserve it; discard bone, if any, and reserve meat in a bowl. Cook shrimp in salted water 5 minutes. Reserve liquid and add

shrimp to cooked fish, also add oysters and crab meat. Keep chilled until ready to use. Combine all liquids to make 3½ pints. In a large, heavy-bottom pot, make a roux. Heat oil, add flour and cook over medium heat, stirring constantly until a deep golden brown. While adding onion, take pot away from heat for fear of burning. Cook until tender. Add tomatoes, celery, garlic, bay leaf, lemon and broth. Return pot to the heat. Raise the heat, stir mixture until it comes to a hard boil. Now add okra, reduce heat to simmer. Cook one hour.

When ready to serve, add fish, crabs, shrimp, oysters, green onion and parsley. Cook 5 minutes longer. Serve in soup plates with hot cooked rice, or with French bread. For extra glamour, add one-fourth cup sherry wine before serving.

*FUN COOKING GUIDE: Be a guest at **your own** party. Prepare gumbo long ahead of serving time-flavor will improve. Heat and add remaining ingredients.One can make sea food gumbo File. Make as above, but omit okra.

Sprinkle ½ teaspoon File herb in each soup plate. Do not add File to the pot. File herb is found in most of the spice shelves in supermarkets. One may omit File and have plain gumbo. All are delicious!

CRAYFISH ÉTOUFFÉE

1 pound cleaned crawfish
   tails (commercial kind)
¼ teaspoon cayenne
   "red pepper"
1 teaspoon salt
Crayfish fat and water to
   make ¾ cup
1 stick margarine or butter

1 medium onion chopped fine
1 heaping teaspoon all purpose
   flour
2 very thin slices lemon
1 heaping tablespoon tomato
   paste
1 tablespoon parsley
1 tablespoon green onion

Use a saucepan with a tight-fitting lid to étouffée. (French for smother). Season crawfish tails with salt and pepper, set aside. Melt butter, add onion; cook over medium heat until tender, stir in the flour, blend well; add water, crayfish fat, lemon, tomato and garlic, cook slowly, about 20 minutes, and add a little more water occasionally. When sauce is done; add crayfish tails, cover with lid. Cook 8 minutes. Season again, to taste. Add green onion and parsley; cook 2 minutes longer. Serve on Steamed rice. Garlic bread and green salad is a good companion to crayfish étouffée.

*FUN COOKING GUIDE: Commercial crayfish are pasteurized and practically cooked. If you are using live crayfish, wash; and scald in boiling water. Clean them, picking off the shells leaving tails whole. Save crayfish fat. When tails and fat from live crayfish are added to cooked mixture, it should be cooked 10 or 15 minutes longer.

FRENCH FRIED SWEET POTATOES

1 or 2 sweet potatoes
1 pint water

1 or 2 teaspoon salt
grease from fried breakfast bacon

Peel and cut sweet potatoes into about ¼ inch thick, soak the slices in the salted water a few minutes, drain. Heat grease 375 degrees, fry potatoes to a golden brown.

*FUN COOKING GUIDE: These fried potatoes make a quick between snack, especially for growing children.

FISH BOUILLABAISSE

(4 Servings)

Poisson Bouillabaisse, a French Acadian version of fish stew, made with almost any kind, or kinds, of fish and vegetables. Originated in Marseilles, France, and brought to our country by Napoleon and his men during the 1800's before the Louisiana Purchase.

A large red fish or red snapper, cut in serving pieces
2 tablespoons olive oil, or cooking oil
¼ cup cooking oil or olive oil
2 large onions, sliced fine
¼ cup celery, chopped fine
1 small can of whole tomatoes, chopped. Use the juice, too
1 teaspoon roux; as above
1 tablespoon tomato sauce

1 carrot, slice thick
2 small, red potatoes. Peel and cut in four
1 bay leaf (optional)
1 tablespoon parsley
2 thin slices of lemon
1 cup water
Salt and red pepper to taste
Season fish generously with salt and red pepper

In a large, heavy-bottom pot, add oil, vegetables, and water; salt and pepper to taste. Place the fish over the top of the vegetables. Put the pot over high heat. When sauce comes to a boil, cover with a tight-fitting lid, reduce heat to very low and cook about one hour. Serve on piping hot, cooked rice. See page 72.

FUN COOKING GUIDE: For a different taste treat, add a small can of mushrooms to the vegetables. Do not use flounder, or pompano. For extra "Nobility" taste-before serving add one-fourth cup sherry wine.

FISH BOUILLABAISSE

(6 Servings)

The following recipe was used by Creole and Cajun people in the Vermillionville and Teche country.

4 pound catfish, clean and cut into serving pieces
Salt and red pepper
½ cup cooking oil

2 large onions, slice fine
4 clove garlic, finely minced
1 large can whole tomatoes
2 thin slices lemon

Season the fish generously with salt and pepper. Place in a covered dish in refrigerator many hours before cooking, this will improve the flavor of the fish.

Combine tomatoes, onion, lemon, and garlic. Using a heavy bottom pot, add oil, place half the fish at bottom. Spread half the tomato mixture over the fish; Repeat with fish and mixture. Place over high heat when it comes to a boil, cover with a tight-fitting cover, reduce the heat to low and let simmer about 2 hours.

Serve with rice as on page 72. Table wine goes well with this dish.

FUN COOKING GUIDE: Many fish may be used, such as bass, red fish, red snapper, gaspergou. But do not use flounder or pompano.

DAD'S CRAB MEAT BURGERS

(Makes four burgers)

1 cup crab meat
¼ cup cooked, mashed potatoes
Salt and pepper to taste
½ a small onion grated, or minced

1 tablespoon finely chopped parsley
2 teaspoons fresh lemon juice
Half an egg shell of well beaten egg

Combine all the ingredients and mix well. Form into flat, round patties, one-half inch thick.

COATING FOR FRYING BURGERS:

¼ cup all purpose flour
Remaining part of beaten egg, mixed with 2 tablespoons of milk

½ cup bread crumbs, or cracker crumbs

Coat burgers on both sides with flour. With finger tips pat on egg mixture, then toss in the crumbs, coating gently. Chill burgers about one hour. Fry in a little hot fat, 375°, turning to brown both sides. Drain on paper toweling. Serves two.

FUN COOKING GUIDE: Salmon croquettes (Croquettes de saumon) can be made the same way as above crab burger. Drain off liquid from a small can of salmon. Do not use the liquid in the croquettes. Shape them like meat balls-may make about 4 croquettes. Make and fry as above.

OREILLE DU COCHON

An Acadian bread so called; because they resemble pig ears. Mama made these delicious treats for us to keep everyone happy on rainy or cold days. They're great fun to make.

1 cup all purpose flour	**⅓ cup water**
¼ teaspoon salt	

Gradually add water to flour and salt, using your finger tips to absorb all the water. Using a little flour, knead, divide into balls. Roll out dough into rounds, paper thin. Roll out all. Fry in deep fat one at a time, using handle of a long wooden spoon, to sink down and hold a few seconds. These resemble pig ears. Coat each with following syrup.

*Fun Cooking Guide: Another version of Creole Oreille du Cochon:

1 cup all purpose flour	**2 melted tablespoons butter**
¼ teaspoon salt	**1 well beaten egg**

Mix and knead - fry each as above - coat with syrup.

SYRUP FOR COATING

1 cup cane syrup	**A pinch of salt**
¼ cup sugar	**1 teaspoon butter**

Boil sugar, syrup and salt over medium low heat, stirring constantly. Take pan away from heat, test in a little cold water. It is right if a few drops form a hard ball. Add butter. Coat each oreille du cochon with syrup.

*FUN COOKING GUIDE: If there is a little leftover syrup in the pan, add a little water and sugar and make candied yam as on page 75.

FRENCH TOAST

Mostly called in Acadian. Country - "Pain Perdu"
(English translation - "Lost Bread")

4 slices stale bread	**A few specks nutmeg (or**
1 egg	**substitute with cinnamon or**
2 tablespoons sugar	**Vanilla Extract)**
¼ cup milk	

Using a small bowl beat egg and sugar until creamy and grains of sugar are dissolved. Add milk. Stir well. Add nutmeg or substitute. Dip each piece of bread, turning to coat each side. DO THIS FAST, there will be some left-over mixture, so dip each piece again, may also pour over all.

Butter a large heavy skillet. Over medium heat brown - turn to brown each side.

Delicious served with coffee, or café au lait, jelly, bacon, or sausage.

*FUN COOKING GUIDE: For a quick breakfast, prepare the night before, will keep if covered in refrigerator. Then cook when needed. This will even improve taste and texture.

CAFÉ AU LAIT

(French for "Coffee Milk")

1 tablespoon sugar	**¼ cup water**
1 cup milk	

In a heavy-bottomed saucepan, over medium heat, add sugar. Cook until sugar .melts then burns to a dark brown, shake pan but do not stir with spoon. Add water, cook until all the sugar is cooked into a syrup, then add milk. Serve hot, as a breakfast beverage,

*FUN COOKING GUIDE: Like New Orleans French Quarter coffee milk, goes well with donuts or oreille du cochon, also with toast and jelly, or peanut butter sandwiches. Double up for more servings.

BANANA PANCAKE

Choose your favorite recipe for the pancakes; or prepare the ready mix kind.

For each serving, cook large pancakes the size of a large skillet. Cook one for each serving, and stack on a platter. (All may be made ahead of time.)

When ready to serve, heat turning once, spread a little softened butter over all. Cut a peeled banana in two lengthwise, sprinkle with a little sugar. Fold over and serve hot.

HOMEMADE FRUIT SYRUPS

1 cup sugar
$\frac{1}{2}$ cup water

$\frac{1}{4}$ cup grape jelly (or substitute)
$\frac{1}{4}$ teaspoon cream of tarter

Combine all the ingredients in a saucepan, cook over medium low heat until syrup comes to a boil. Pour mixture in container. Delicious served with pancakes, biscuits, or bread and butter, for a sweet tooth, or a snack.

*FUN COOKING GUIDE: This fruit syrup can be made with any fruit jelly, especially if only a small amount remains in jar.

HOMEMADE MAPLE SYRUP

$\frac{1}{4}$ teaspoon cream of tarter
1 cup sugar
$\frac{1}{2}$ cup water

1 or 2 drops mapleine (available in most supermarkets)

Cook as above fruit syrup. Serve with biscuits or hotcakes.

*FUN COOKING GUIDE: If crystals appear, days after using - moments before using, place the container in a pan of water, heat a few minutes, and crystals will dissolve.

PECAN DATE PIE

One 9 inch unbaked pie crust
$\frac{3}{4}$ cup butter
$\frac{3}{4}$ cup brown sugar
2 egg yolks
$\frac{1}{2}$ cup evaporated milk

2 egg whites
$\frac{3}{4}$ cup chopped pecans
1 cup dates
$\frac{1}{8}$ teaspoon clove powder
$\frac{1}{4}$ teaspoon cinnamon powder

Cream butter, add sugar and beat until creamy. Add egg yolks one at a time. Blend in milk, spices, pecans, and dates.

Beat egg whites until stiff, and fold into mixture. Pour into pie crust and spread evenly. Bake 40 minutes at 350-degree oven. Serve with whipped cream.

*FUN COOKING GUIDE: May make into small individual tarts instead of large pie.

GATEAU du SYRUP
(Syrup Cake)

½ cup butter
½ cup brown sugar
2 eggs
1 cup Louisiana cane syrup
½ cup milk
1 teaspoon grated orange rind
½ teaspoon soda

1 tablespoon vinegar
Sift together
  2½ cups flour
  3 teaspoons baking powder
  ½ teaspoon nutmeg
  ½ teaspoon ginger or cinnamon

Cream butter and sugar, add eggs, grated orange, beat well. Gradually add flour alternately with milk and syrup ending with flour mixture. Combine vinegar and soda. Fold into cake mixture.

Pour cooking oil and spread into bake pan, place a sheet of wax paper, press well. Then quickly turn over wax paper. Pour cake mixture. Bake 350° in oven about 45 minutes.

Good served warm. My Mother served this cake usually for dessert after a Friday fish dinner.

*FUN COOKING GUIDE: For a different taste treat, add raisins or pecans to cake batter before baking.

BASIC RECIPE FOR FRUIT TARTS

We in Louisiana make these tarts with blackberry, pear, or fig preserves.

2 heaping tablespoons butter or
  margarine
1¼ cups sugar
2 well beaten eggs
1 teaspoon vanilla extract

⅓ cup milk
3¼ cups all purpose flour. DO NOT
  USE SELF-RISING FLOUR
3 teaspoons baking powder
½ teaspoon salt

Sift together flour, baking powder, and salt. Cream butter, sugar, and vanilla - add eggs, and beat well. Add flour mixture alternately with milk, ending with flour; knead. Chill the dough.

Turn out dough on lightly floured surface; knead with heel of the hand, about 20 strokes. Use 2 sheets wax paper to work on.

Divide dough into portions. Roll out into circles ¼ inch thick, spoon out preserves on half the round, fold over, prick around moon shape with a fork. Place on cookie sheet and bake for about 15 minutes.

*FUN BAKING GUIDE: When I bake tarts or cookies, I always line cookie sheet with brown paper, then wax paper, grease, because pastries sometimes have a tendency to burn.

*FUN COOKING GUIDE: Besides the berry, fig, and pear preserves, you may use your favorite jam or jelly, also coconut custard. The dough can be made into cookies - including nuts.

FESTIVE RED CAKE

(Cake may be used on Christmas, New Year's or Valentine's Day)

$\frac{1}{2}$ cup butter or margarine	1 cup buttermilk
1 cup sugar	2 heaping tablespoons cocoa
2 eggs well beaten	2 ounces red food coloring
1 teaspoon vanilla extract	1 teaspoon soda
2$\frac{1}{4}$ cups all purpose flour	1 tablespoon vinegar
$\frac{1}{2}$ teaspoon salt	

Preheat oven to 350 degrees. Grease 2 nine-inch cake pans. Combine butter, sugar, and vanilla and beat until creamy. Add eggs. Add flour, salt, and buttermilk alternately. Beat until smooth. In a cup, combine a little batter with cocoa and food coloring; mix well. Add to the batter. Add soda to the vinegar (it will foam) so quickly fold into the batter. Pour into pans, bake 30 to 35 minutes, until surface of the cake springs back when pressed with finger tips. Let cool in pan; invert; split cakes in two to make four layers. Frost with cream filling.

CREAM FILLING

Combine 1 cup of milk with 3 tablespoons flour. Cook over low heat, stirring constantly until thick and smooth. Cool. Cream together 1 cup sugar with 1 cup margarine. Beat until granules disappear; gradually add cooled milk mixture. Beat until consistency of whipped cream. Frost cake.

*FUN COOKING GUIDE: The recipe for this cake can be made into a devil's food cake by omitting red food coloring, also can make a gold cake.

❖ *Index* ❖

B-Q'd Chicken, 139; Banana Pancake, 146; Basic Recipe for Fruit Tarts, 148; Café au Lait, 146; Chicken Spaghetti, 136; Cornichon de Mirliton, 135; Crayfish Etouffée, 142; Dad's Crab Meat Burgers, 144; Festive Red Cake, 149; Fish Bouillabaisse, 143, 144; French Fried Sweet Potatoes, 142; French Toast, 146; Gateau du Syrup, 148; Homemade Fruit Syrups, 147; Homemade Maple Syrup, 147; Margaret's Two-in-One Bar-B-Q Sauce, 138; Oreille du Cochon, 145; Oyster Spaghetti, Cajun Style, 137; Pecan Date Pie, 147; Remoulade Sauce for Shrimp, 136; Roux, 140; Rum Balls, 135; Sauce Piquante, 137; Sauce to Darken Gravies, 140; Seafood and Okra Gumbo, 141; Shrimp Jambalaya, 138; Sour Cream Dressing for Baked Potatoes, 136

Lamb à la Louisiane, 63

Lamb Patties, 64

Leftover Dishes: 76-83; Beef and Eggplant Casserole, 76; Casserole with Leftover Vegetables, 79; Chicken Croquettes, 76; Corn Beef Hash, 77; Egg Sauce, 78; Ground Meat Hash, 78; Ham Croquettes, 77; Ham Hash, 78; Irish Potato Surprise, 79; Pork and Noodle Casserole, 80; Rice, Blackeyed Peas and Ham Dressing, 83; Rice, Cabbage and Ham Dressing, 83; Turkey Stew, 80; Turkey Bone Gumbo, 82; Turkey Soufflés with Giblet Gravy, 82; Turkey Treat on Toast, 81

Lily's Corn Bread Dressing, 38

Lime and Fruit Jell-O, 115

Louisiana French Oyster Loaf, 27

Maquechou, 93

Margaret's Two-in-One Bar-B-Q Sauce, 138

Marinated Cucumber Slices, 118

Marinated Green Beans, 114

Meat and Vegetable Combinations: 67-75; Creole Cabbage Rolls, 68; Eggplant and Meat Roll in Sauce, 69; Smothered Beef and Carrots, 70; Smothered Ham and Cabbage, 70; Stuffed Cabbage Head, 67; Stuffed Mirlitons, 71; Stuffed Peppers, 72; Stuffed Tomatoes, 72; Stuffed White Squash, 74; Top-of-Stove Bell Pepper Dressing, 74

Meatball Surprise with Gravy, 50

Milk Gravy, 41

Mom's Skillet Sausage in White Wine, 63

Purple Cabbage with Apples,
87
Purple Pickled Eggs, 117

Quick Bread Puffs, 125

Raisin Sauce for Ham, 65
Red Bean Salad, 110
Red Beans and Rice, 84
Remoulade Sauce for Shrimp,
136
Rice and Salmon Casserole, 17
Rice, Blackeyed Peas and Ham
Dressing, 83
Rice, Cabbage and Ham
Dressing, 83
Ripe Olive Hot Slaw, 109
Roast Beef Supreme, 51
Roux, 140
Rum Balls, 135
Rum Sauce, 134

Salads: 109-18; Apple Raisin
Salad, 110; Beets in Orange
Sauce, 118; Cabbage Beet
Relish, 115; Candlestick
Salad, 109; Carrot and
Coconut Health Salad, 111;
Country-Style Beets and
Potato Salad, 118; Dill Sour
Green Beans, 114; Fruit
Combinations, 110; German
Potato Salad, 113; Grape
and Cabbage Salad, 113; Hot
Potato Salad, 113; Lime and
Fruit Jell-O, 115; Marinated
Cucumber Slices, 118;
Marinated Green Beans,

114; Orange and Coconut
Compote, 111; Pear and
Grape Salad on Lettuce, 112;
Pickled Baby Okra, 116;
Pickled Beets, 116; Pickled
Carrots, 116; Pickled White
Summer Squash, 116;
Pineapple Chunks with Sour
Cream, 111; Pineapple Slaw,
112; Pineapple Slices Stuffed
with Grape Cream Cheese,
112; Pink Onion Rings, 117;
Pink Onion Rings, Orange
Slices, and Green Grapes,
117; Purple Pickled Eggs,
117; Red Bean Salad, 110;
Ripe Olive Hot Slaw, 109;
Serving Cantaloupe, 110;
Spiced Stuffed Prunes and
Apricots, 112
Sauce for Green Beans, 114
Sauce Piquante, 137
Sauce to Darken Gravies, 140
Sauces: 65-66; Horseradish
Sauce, 66; Raisin Sauce for
Ham, 65
Sausage à-la-Creole, 62
Seafood and Okra Gumbo, 141
Seafood Casserole, 29
Serving Cantaloupe, 110
Shrimp and Okra Gumbo, 30
Shrimp and Oyster Dressing,
16
Shrimp Creole, 30
Shrimp Jambalaya, 138
Shrimp à la Louisiane, 32
Shrimpboat Cocktail, 26
Smothered Beef and Carrots, 70